*Buddha Mind, Buddha Body*

# Buddha Mind, Buddha Body

## Thich Nhat Hanh

PARALLAX PRESS
BERKELEY, CALIFORNIA

Parallax Press
P.O. Box 7355
Berkeley, California 94707
www.parallax.org

Parallax Press is the publishing division of Unified Buddhist Church, Inc.

Edited by Rachel Neumann.
Cover design by Jess Morphew.
Text design by Gopa&Ted2, Inc.

Library of Congress Cataloging-in-Publication Data

Nhât Hanh, Thích.
  Buddha mind, Buddha body / Thich Nhat Hanh.
     p. cm.
  ISBN 978-1-888375-75-6
  1. Spiritual life—Buddhism. 2. Meditation—Buddhism. I. Title.
  BQ9800.T5392N4543 2007
  294.3'444—dc22
                       2007009396

3 4 5 6 7 / 12 11 10 09 08

# Contents

# Foreword

T HE COMPELLING SUMMARY image for this wonderfully comforting and inspiring book comes in its opening pages. Say you are struggling with a computer problem. Your older brother arrives as you are about to give up and says, "Move over. I'll take over a little." You are reassured even before the problem is solved.

That big brother is the Buddha within each of us, our clearest understanding. And Thich Nhat Hanh, with his friendly, patient, steadfast, confident, contemporary and often witty voice, seems, to me, an intermediary big brother. On each page of this book, he talks directly to us, saying, "Look! Right there within you is the very wisdom that leads to compassion."

This is a small book, but everything is in it is articulated with poetry, with traditional Buddhist images, with religious vocabulary from western tradition. That it should be about everything, and presented in universalistic language, is completely consistent with its underlying message: There is nothing at all separate from all that is. Interbeing is all there is. It's impossible to read this book without being inspired to redouble one's efforts on behalf of other people, on behalf of all beings, and on behalf of the planet, knowing these efforts will also lead to our own happiness.

—Sylvia Boorstein

*Buddha Mind, Buddha Body*

# 1

## Two Feet, One Mind

I N THE LOTUS SUTRA, the Buddha is described as the most respected
and loved creature who walked on two feet. He was so loved because he
knew how to enjoy a good walk. Walking is an important form of Buddhist meditation. It can be a very deep spiritual practice. But when the Buddha walked, he walked without effort. He just enjoyed walking. He didn't
have to strain, because when you walk in mindfulness, you are in touch
with the all the wonders of life within you and around you. This is the best
way to practice, with the appearance of non-practice. You don't make any
effort, you don't struggle, you just enjoy walking, but it's very deep. "My
practice," the Buddha said, "is the practice of non-practice, the attainment
of non-attainment."*

For many of us, the idea of practice without effort, of the relaxed pleasure of mindfulness, seems very difficult. That is because we don't walk with
our feet. Of course, physically our feet are doing the walking, but because
our minds are elsewhere, we are not walking with our full body and our full
consciousness. We see our minds and our bodies as two separate things.
While our bodies are walking one way, our consciousness is tugging us in
a different direction.

For the Buddha, mind and the body are two aspects of the same thing.
Walking is as simple as putting one foot in front of the other. But we often
find it difficult or tedious. We drive a few blocks rather than walk in order
to "save time." When we understand the interconnectedness of our bodies

* This line is in the Sutra of Forty-two Chapters, the first sutra introduced into China and
Vietnam from India.

and our minds, the simple act of walking like the Buddha can feel supremely easy and pleasurable.

## WALKING LIKE A BUDDHA

You can make a step and touch the earth in such a way that you establish yourself in the present moment, and you will arrive in the here and the now. You don't need to make any effort at all. Your foot touches the earth mindfully, and you arrive firmly in the here and the now. And suddenly you are free—free from all projects, all worries, all expectations. You are fully present, fully alive, and you are touching the earth.

When you practice slow walking meditation alone, you may like to try this: Breathe in and take one step, and focus all your attention on the sole of your foot. If you have not arrived fully, one hundred percent in the here and the now, don't make the next step. You have the luxury of doing this. Then when you're sure that you've arrived one hundred percent in the here and the now, touching reality deeply, then you smile and you make the next step. When you walk like this, you print your stability, your solidity, your freedom, your joy on the ground. Your foot is like a seal, the seal of the emperor. When you put the seal on a piece of paper, the seal makes an impression. Looking in your footstep, what do we see? We see the mark of freedom, the mark of solidity, the mark of happiness, the mark of life. I'm sure you can make a step like that, because there is a Buddha in you. It's called the Buddha nature, the capacity of being aware of what is going on. What's going on is: I am alive, I am making a step. A person, a human being, Homo sapiens should be able to do this. There is a Buddha in every one of us, and we should allow the Buddha to walk.

Even in the most difficult situation, you can walk like a Buddha. Last year, in the month of March, we were visiting Korea, and there was one moment when we were surrounded by hundreds of people. Each of them had a camera, and they were closing in. There was no path to walk, and everyone was aiming their camera at us. It was a very difficult situation in which to do walking meditation. And I said, "Dear Buddha, I give up, you walk for me." And right away the Buddha came, and he walked, with complete freedom. And then the crowd just made room for the Buddha to walk; no effort was made.

If you find yourself in some difficulty, step aside, and allow the Buddha to take your place. The Buddha *is* in you. This works in all situations. I have tried it. It's like encountering a problem when you're using the computer. You can't get out of the situation. But then your big brother who is very skillful with computers comes along and says, "Move over a little, I'll take over." And as soon as he sits down, everything is all right. It's like that. When you find it difficult, withdraw and allow the Buddha to take place. It's very easy. And for me it always works. You have to have faith in the Buddha within, and allow the Buddha to walk, and also allow the people dear to you to walk.

When you walk, who do you walk for? You can walk to get somewhere but you can also walk as a kind of meditative offering. It's very nice to walk for your parents or for your grandparents who may not have known the practice of walking in mindfulness. You ancestors may have spent their whole life without the chance to make a peaceful, happy steps and establish themselves fully in the present moment. This is a great pity, but we do not need to repeat this situation.

It is possible for you to walk with the feet of your mother. Poor mother, she didn't have much opportunity to walk like this. You can say, "Mother, would you like to walk with me?" And then you walk with her, and your heart will fill with love. You free yourself and you free her at the same time, because it's true that your mother is in you, in every cell of your body. Your father is also fully present in every cell of your body. You can say, "Dad, would you like to join me?" Then suddenly you walk with the feet of your father. It's a joy. It's very rewarding. And I assure you that it's not difficult. You don't have to fight and struggle in order to do it. Just become aware, and everything will go well.

After you have been able to walk for your dear ones, you can walk for the people who have made your life miserable. You can walk for those who have attacked you, who have destroyed your home, your country, and your people. These people weren't happy. They didn't have enough love for themselves and for other people. They have made your life miserable, and the life of your family and your people miserable. And there will be a time when you'll be able to walk for them too. Walking like that, you become a Buddha, you become a bodhisattva filled with love, understanding, and compassion.

# 2

## How the Mind Works

B EFORE WE CAN WALK for our ancestors, before we can walk for
those who have harmed us, we need to learn how to walk for ourselves. To do that, we need to understand our minds and the connection between our feet and our heads. The Vietnamese Zen Master
Thuong Chieu said, "When we understand how our mind works, our practice becomes easy." In other words, if we can walk mindfully with our consciousness, our feet will naturally follow.

The Buddha taught that consciousness is always continuing, like a
stream of water. There are four kinds of consciousness: mind consciousness, sense consciousness, store consciousness, and *manas*. Sometimes,
these four kinds of consciousness are considered eight, with sense consciousness being divided into five (eyes, ears, mouth, nose, touch). When
we walk mindfully, all four layers of consciousness are operating.

Mind consciousness is the first kind of consciousness. It uses up most of
our energy. Mind consciousness is our "working" consciousness that
makes judgments and plans; it is the part of our consciousness that worries
and analyzes. When we speak of mind consciousness, we're also speaking
of body consciousness, because mind consciousness isn't possible without
the brain. Body and mind are simply two aspects of the same thing. Body
without consciousness is not a real, live body. And consciousness can't
manifest itself without a body.

It's possible for us to train ourselves to remove the false distinction
between brain and consciousness. We shouldn't say that consciousness is
born from the brain, because the opposite is true: the brain is born from

consciousness. The brain is only two percent of the body's weight, but it consumes twenty percent of the body's energy. So using mind consciousness is very expensive. Thinking, worrying, and planning take a lot of energy.

We can economize the energy by training our mind consciousness in the habit of mindfulness. Mindfulness keeps us in the present moment and allows our mind consciousness to relax and let go of the energy of worrying about the past or predicting the future.

The second level of consciousness is sense consciousness, the consciousness that comes from our five senses: sight, hearing, taste, touch, and smell. When we walk, we use this kind of consciousness as well. We see in front of us, we taste and smell the air, we hear sounds and our feet touch the ground. We sometimes call these senses "gates," or "doors," because all objects of perception enter consciousness through our sensory contact with them. Sense consciousness always involves three elements: first, the sense organ (eyes, ears, nose, tongue, or body); second, the sense object itself (the object we're smelling or the sound we're hearing); and finally, our experience of what we are seeing, hearing, smelling, tasting, or touching.

The third layer of consciousness, store consciousness, is the deepest. There are many names for this kind of consciousness. In the Mahayana tradition this is called store consciousness, or *alaya* in Sanskrit. The Theravada tradition uses the Pali word *bhavanga* to describe this consciousness. Bhavanga means constantly flowing, like a river. Store consciousness is also sometimes called root consciousness (*mulavijñana* in Sanskrit) or *sarvabijaka*, which means "the totality of the seeds." In Vietnamese, we call store consciousness *tang*. Tang means to keep and preserve.

These different names hint at the three aspects of store consciousness. The first meaning is of a place, a "store," where all kinds of seeds and information are kept. A mustard seed is very small. But if the mustard seed has the opportunity to sprout, the outer shell will break, and what is very small inside will become very big—a huge plant of mustard. In the Gospels there is the image of a mustard seed that has the capacity to become a huge tree where many birds can come and take refuge.* The mustard seed is the sym-

* Matthew 13:31; Mark 4:31; Luke 13:19

bol of the contents of store consciousness. Everything we see or touch has a seed lying deep in store consciousness.

The second meaning is suggested by the Vietnamese name tang, because store consciousness doesn't just take in all the information, it holds it and preserves it. The third meaning is suggested by bhavanga, the sense of processing and transforming.

Store consciousness is like a museum. A museum can only be called a museum when there are things in it. When there is nothing in it, you can call it a building, but not a museum. The conservator is the one who is responsible for the museum. Her function is to keep the various objects preserved and not allow them to be stolen. But there must be things to be stored, things to be kept. Store consciousness refers to the storing and also to what is stored—that is, all the information from the past, from our ancestors, and all the information received from the other consciousnesses. In Buddhist tradition, this information is stored as *bija*, seeds.

Suppose this morning you hear a certain chant for the first time. Your ear and the music come together and provoke the manifestation of the mental formation called touch, which causes store consciousness to vibrate. That information, a new seed, falls into the store continuum. Store consciousness has the capacity to receive the seed and store it in its heart. Store consciousness preserves all the information it receives. But the function of store consciousness isn't just to receive and store these seeds; its job is also to process this information.

The work of processing on this level is not expensive. Store consciousness doesn't spend as much energy as, for example, mind consciousness. Store consciousness can process this information without a lot of work on your part. So if you want to save your energy, don't think too much, don't plan too much, and don't worry too much. Allow your store consciousness to do most of the processing.

Store consciousness operates in the absence of mind consciousness. It can do a lot of things. It can do a lot of planning; it can make a lot of decisions without your knowing about it. When we go into a department store and look for a hat or a shirt, we have the impression, while looking at the items displayed, that we have free will and that, finances permitting, we are free to choose whatever we want. If the vendor asks us what we like, we can point to or verbalize the object of our desire. And we likely have the impression that we are free people at this moment, using our mind consciousness to select things that we like. But that is an illusion. Everything has been decided already in store consciousness. At that moment we are caught; we are not free people. Our sense of beauty, our sense of liking or disliking, has been decided very certainly and very discreetly on the level of store consciousness.

It's an illusion that we are free. The degree of freedom that our mind consciousness has is actually very small. Store consciousness dictates many of the things we do, because store consciousness continuously receives, embraces, maintains, processes, and makes many decisions without the participation of mind consciousness. But if we know the practice, we can influence our store consciousness; we can help influence how our store consciousness stores and processes information so as to make better decisions. We can influence it.

Just like mind consciousness and sense consciousness, store consciousness consumes. When you are around a group of people, although you want to be yourself, you are consuming their ways, and you are consuming their store consciousness. Our consciousness is fed with other consciousnesses. The way we make decisions, our likes and dislikes, depend on the collective way of seeing things. You may not see something as beautiful, but if many people think that it's beautiful, then slowly you may come to accept it as beautiful also, because the individual consciousness is made up of collective consciousness.

The value of the dollar is made up of the collective thinking of people, not just of objective economic elements. People's fears, desires, and expectations make the dollar go up and go down. We are influenced by the collective ways of seeing and thinking. That's why selecting the people you are around is very important. It's very important to surround yourself with people who have loving kindness, understanding, and compassion, because day and night we are influenced by the collective consciousness.

Store consciousness offers us enlightenment and transformation. This possibility is contained in its third meaning, its always-flowing nature.

Store consciousness is like a garden where we can plant the seeds of flowers, fruits, and vegetables, and then flowers, fruits, and vegetables will grow. Mind consciousness is only a gardener. A gardener can help the land and take care of the land, but the gardener has to believe in the land, believe that it can offer us fruits, flowers, and vegetables. As practitioners, we can't rely on our mind consciousness alone; we have to rely on our store consciousness as well. Decisions are being made down there.

Suppose you type something on your computer and this information is stored on the hard drive. That hard drive is like store consciousness. Although the information doesn't appear on the screen, it is still there. You only need to click and it will manifest. The bija, the seeds in store consciousness, are like the data you store on your computer. If you want to, you can click and help it appear on the screen of mind consciousness. Mind consciousness is like a screen and store consciousness is like the hard drive, because it can store a lot in it. Store consciousness has the capacity of storing, maintaining, and preserving information so that it can't be erased.

Unlike information on a hard drive, however, all the seeds are of an organic nature and they can be modified. The seed of hatred, for example, can be weakened and its energy can be transformed into the energy of compassion. The seed of love can be watered and strengthened. The nature of the information that's being kept and processed by the store consciousness is always flowing and always changing. Love can be transformed into hate, and hate can be transformed back into love.

Store consciousness is also a victim. It's an object of attachment; it's not free. In store consciousness there are elements of ignorance—delusion, anger, fear—and these elements form a force of energy that clings, that wants to possess. This is the fourth level of consciousness, called manas, which I like to translate as "cogitation." Manas consciousness has at its root the belief in a separate self, the belief in a person. This consciousness, the feeling and instinct called "I am," is very deeply seated in store consciousness. It's not a view taken up by mind consciousness. Deeply seated in the depths of store consciousness is this idea that there is a self that is separate from nonself elements. The function of manas is to cling to store consciousness as a separate self.

Another way of thinking of manas is as *adana* consciousness. Adana means "appropriation." Imagine that a vine puts forth a shoot, and then the shoot turns back and embraces and encircles the trunk of the tree. This deep-seated delusion—the belief that there is a self—is there in store consciousness as the result of ignorance and fear, and it gives rise to an energy that turns around and embraces store consciousness and makes it the only object of its love.

Manas is always operating. It never lets go of store consciousness. It's always embracing, always holding or sticking to store consciousness. It believes store consciousness to be the object of its love. That's why store consciousness isn't free. There's an illusion that store consciousness is "me," is my beloved, so I can't let it go. Day and night there's a secret, deep cogitation that this is me, this is mine, and I have to do everything I can to grasp, to protect, to make it mine. Manas is born and rooted in store consciousness. It arises from store consciousness and it turns around and embraces store consciousness as its object: "You are my beloved, you are me." The function of manas is to appropriate store consciousness as its own.

## How the Four Consciousnessess Interact

Now we have the names of the four layers of consciousness and we can see how they interact. Buddhism sometimes speaks of store consciousnesses as the ocean of consciousness and the other consciousnesses are described as waves rising from the base of the ocean. There's a wind, and that wind provokes the other consciousnesses to manifest.

Store consciousness is the foundation, the root. From this base, the mind manifests and operates. Sometimes it rests and comes home to store consciousness. In this way, store consciousness is the garden and mind consciousness the gardener. Manas also springs from store consciousness, but then turns around and embraces store consciousness as its property, as an object of its love. It does this day and night. That is why it's called the lover.

When you fall in love with someone, you don't really fall in love with him or her. You create an image that is quite different from reality. After living with him for one or two years, you discover that the image that you have of him is quite far away from the reality. Although manas is born from store consciousness, her way of looking at store consciousness is full of illusions and wrong perceptions. She creates an image of store as the object of her love, and this object is not exactly the reality. When we use a camera to take a picture of someone, the picture is only an image, it's not that person. The lover thinks that it loves store, but actually it only loves the image she herself has created. An object of consciousness can either be the thing in itself, or it can be a representation that you fabricate subjectively.

So we have the gardener, mind, and we have the lover, manas. But mind consciousness may be interrupted. For example, when we sleep without dreaming, mind consciousness is not operating. When we're in a coma, mind consciousness stops working completely. And there are deep concentrations when mind consciousness completely stops operating—there's no thinking, no planning, nothing—yet store consciousness continues to operate. Deep walking meditation can be like this. Your body is moving and your store consciousness continues to be working, but you are not aware of it.

Mind consciousness can also operate independently from sense consciousnesses or it can operate in collaboration. Suppose you're invited into an exhibition. Standing in front of a painting, eye consciousness is operating. The first moment, maybe, eye consciousness is looking at the artwork without any thinking, any judgment. But seeing the object in and of itself lasts for only one *kshana,* one brief moment. Very soon the experiences come up and mind consciousness comes up with all kinds of evaluations and judgment and things like that. That is a cooperation between the two kinds of consciousness: mind consciousness and eye consciousness. When mind consciousness is working with sense consciousness, it's called associative consciousness. If you are absorbed in deep reflection, you don't see, you don't hear, you don't touch anymore. In that deep place of reflection, mind consciousness is working alone. In meditation you usually use independent mind consciousness. We close our eyes, we close our ears, we don't want to be disturbed by what we see or hear. The concentration is being performed by mind consciousness alone.

There are also times when sense consciousness operates in collaboration with store consciousness without going through the mind. It's funny, but it happens very, very often. When you drive your car, you are able to avoid many accidents, even if your mind consciousness is thinking of other things. You may not even be thinking of driving at all. And yet, most of the time at least, you don't get into an accident. When you walk, you rarely trip (or at least only occasionally!). This is because the impressions and images provided by eye consciousness are received by store consciousness, and decisions are made without ever going through mind consciousness. When someone suddenly holds something close to your eyes—for instance, if someone is about to hit you, or when something is about to fall on you—you react quickly. That quick reaction, that decision, is not made by mind consciousness. If you have to make a quick maneuver, it's not your mind consciousness that does it. We don't think, "Oh, there is a rock, therefore I have to step over it." We just do it. That instinct of self-defense comes from store consciousness.

I had a dream once that illustrates this point. In Asia, in olden times, we had to prepare our own rice from the paddy. We had to remove the husk from the rice kernel before we could cook and eat the rice. In the temple we had an instrument that removed the husk. The action of removing the husk had a very particular, rhythmic kind of sound. One day I was taking a nap, about one thirty in the afternoon, because in Asia at that time it's very hot and you have the tendency to take a nap for half an hour before you resume your activities. During the time that I was napping I heard the sound of husking. But in fact it was a student of mine scraping a block of Chinese ink. In order to have ink to write with a brush you had to put some water on a plate and scrape the solid block of ink into the water. That sound somehow found a way to go through my ear consciousness into store consciousness and was transmitted to mind consciousness. That is why in my dream I saw someone husking rice. But in fact it was not husking, it was only the preparation of the ink. So the impression comes in two ways: through the way of mind consciousness or through the way of store consciousness. And everything that goes through the five sense consciousnesses can be stored, can be analyzed, can be processed by store consciousness. They do not have to go through mind consciousness always. They can go directly from the first five consciousnesses to store consciousness.

In a cold room at night, even though you're not dreaming, and mind consciousness isn't functioning, the feeling of cold still penetrates into the body at the level of sense consciousness. This makes a vibration on the level of store consciousness, and your body moves the blanket up to cover you.

Whether we're driving, manipulating a machine, or performing other tasks, many of us allow our sense consciousness to collaborate with store consciousness, which enables us to do many things without the intervention of mind consciousness. When we bring our mind consciousness into this work, then suddenly we may become aware of the mental formations that are arising.

The word "formation" (*samskara* in Sanskrit) means something that manifests when many conditions come together. When we look at a flower, we can recognize many of the elements that have come together to make the flower manifest in that form. We know that without the rain there can be no water and the flower cannot manifest. And we see that the sunshine is also there. The earth, the compost, the gardener, time, space, and many elements came together to help this flower manifest. The flower doesn't have a separate existence; it's a formation. The sun, the moon, the mountain, and the river are all formations. Using the word "formation" reminds us that there is no separate core of existence in them. There is only a coming together of many, many conditions for something to manifest.

As Buddhist practitioners, we can train ourselves to look at everything as a formation. We know that all formations are changing all the time. Impermanence is one of the marks of reality, because everything changes.

## MENTAL FORMATIONS

Formations that exist in consciousness are called mental formations. When there's contact between a sense organ (eyes, ears, nose, mouth, body) and an object, sense consciousness arises. And at the moment your eyes first gaze on an object, or you first feel the wind on your skin, the first mental formation of contact manifests. Contact causes a vibration on the level of store consciousness.

If the impression is weak, then the vibration stops and the current of store consciousness recovers its tranquility; you continue to sleep or you continue with your activities, because that impression created by touch has not been strong enough to draw the attention of mind consciousness. It's like when a flying insect lands on the surface of the water and causes the water to ripple a little bit. After the insect flies off, the surface of the water becomes completely calm again. So although the mental formation manifests, although the current of the life continuum vibrates, there's no awareness born in mind consciousness because the impression is too weak.

Sometimes in Buddhist psychology, one speaks of forty-nine or fifty mental formations. In my tradition, we speak of fifty-one. The fifty-one mental formations are also called mental concomitants; that is, they are the very content of consciousness, the way the drops of water are the very content of the river. For example, anger is a mental formation. Mind consciousness can operate in such a way that anger can manifest in mind consciousness. In that moment, mind consciousness is filled with anger, and we may feel our mind consciousness is nothing but anger. But in fact, mind consciousness is not just anger, because later on compassion arises, and at that time, mind consciousness becomes compassion. Mind consciousness is, at various times, all fifty-one mental formations, be they positive, negative, or neutral.

Without mental formations, there can't be consciousness. It's as if we're discussing a formation of birds. The formation holds the birds together, and they fly beautifully in the sky. You don't need someone to hold the birds and keep them flying in one formation. You don't need a self to create the formation. The birds just do it. In a beehive, you don't need someone who gives the order for this bee to go left and that bee to go right; they just communicate among themselves and are a beehive. Among all the bees, every bee may have a different responsibility, but no bee claims to be the boss of all the bees, not even the queen. The queen is not the boss. Her function is simply to give birth to the eggs. If you have a good community, a good *Sangha,* it's like this beehive in which all the parts make up the whole, with no leader, no boss.

When we say it's raining, we mean that raining is taking place. You don't need someone up above to perform the raining. It's not that there is the rain, and there is the one who causes the rain to fall. In fact, when you say the rain is falling, it's very funny, because if it weren't falling, it wouldn't be rain. In our way of speaking, we're used to having a subject and a verb. That's why we need the word "it" when we say, "it rains." "It" is the subject, the one who makes the rain possible. But, looking deeply, we don't need a "rainer," we just need the rain. Raining and the rain are the same. The formation of birds and the birds are the same—there's no "self," no boss involved.

There's a mental formation called *vitarka,* "initial thought." When we use the verb "to think" in English, we need a subject of the verb: I think, you think, he thinks. But, really, you don't need a subject for a thought to be produced. Thinking without a thinker—it's absolutely possible. To think is to think about something. To perceive is to perceive something. The perceiver and the object that is perceived are one.

When Descartes said, "I think, therefore I am," his point was that if I think, there must be an "I" for thinking to be possible. When he made the declaration "I think," he believed that he could demonstrate that the "I" exists. We have the strong habit of believing in a self. But, observing very deeply, we can see that a thought does not need a thinker to be possible. There is no thinker behind the thinking—there is just the thinking; that's enough.

Now, if Mr. Descartes were here, we might ask him, "Monsieur Descartes, you say, 'You think, therefore you are.' But what are you? You are your thinking. Thinking—that's enough. Thinking manifests without the need of a self behind it."

Thinking without a thinker. Feeling without a feeler. What is our anger without our "self"? This is the object of our meditation. All the fifty-one mental formations take place and manifest without a self behind them arranging for this to appear, and then for that to appear. Our mind consciousness is in the habit of basing itself on the idea of self, on *manas.* But we can meditate to be more aware of our store consciousness, where we keep the seeds of all those mental formations that are not currently manifesting in our mind.

When we meditate, we practice looking deeply in order to bring light and clarity into our way of seeing things. When the vision of no-self is obtained, our delusion is removed. This is what we call transformation. In the Buddhist tradition, transformation is possible with deep understanding. The moment the vision of no-self is there, manas, the elusive notion of "I am," disintegrates, and we find ourselves enjoying, in this very moment, freedom and happiness.

# 3

## Finding Your Mind

W HEN WE ARE stressed about something, or very busy, we often say we're "losing our minds." But where were they before they were lost and where did they go to? In the Surangama Sutra, a popular Buddhist text in Vietnam and China, the Buddha and his disciple Ananda discuss how to locate the mind. Is it inside the body, outside the body, or in between the body and the world outside? Ultimately, the sutra teaches us that mind is non-local. In other words, you cannot say that it is inside the body, outside the body, or in between. It doesn't have one set location.

Not only is the mind not localized, but everything is like this. This morning I picked a tender green leaf off the ground. Is this leaf in my mind or outside of it? What a question! It's a very simple question, but very difficult to answer. The notion of outside and inside cannot be applied to reality.

We tend to think of the mind as "in here" and the world as "out there," the mind as subjective and the world, the body, as objective. The Buddha taught that mind and object of mind do not exist separately, they inter-are. Without this, the other cannot be. There is no perceiver without the perceived. Object and subject manifest together. Usually when we think of mind, we think only of mind consciousness. But mind is not just mind consciousness, it is also manas, it is also store consciousness.

We can train ourselves to look at our body as a river, and our mind as part of that same river, always flowing, always changing. According to Buddhist psychology, the greatest obstacle to our ability to see reality clearly is our tendency to get tangled in the notion that subject is something different from object, and that object is something independent from the subject. This way of looking has become a habit, a pattern influencing our thinking and behavior.

When I was a young novice, we learned that consciousness has three parts. The first and second parts are: the *darshana*, the perceiver; and the *nimita*, the perceived—that is, the subject and object. The subject and object lean on each other in order to manifest. If you believe that the subject can be there without the object, that is the greatest kind of error. We have the tendency to believe that the subject of cognition, our mind, is something that can exist separately and independently from the object of cognition or the object of experience. And we believe that the object of cognition, what is out there, is something that exists separately from the subject of cognition.

In Buddhism there is the term *namarupa*.* Namarupa is equivalent to psychosoma. Reality manifests in a double aspect, psyche and soma, mental and biological. And one cannot be without the other. Brain and mind are two aspects of the manifestation of one thing. So we must train ourselves to look at the brain as consciousness, and not to see consciousness as something totally separated and different from the brain.

When you invite the flame to manifest, you may think that the flame is something totally different from the match. But you know that the flame is immanent, is hidden in the fuel of the match head, is hidden in the oxygen in the air; the flame has no real locality. And when conditions come together, the flame manifests. The nature of consciousness is also nonlocal. We know that consciousness is always consciousness of something. Object and subject are always together. Looking into this part, you see the other part. Looking into the other part, you see this part. That is the nature of interbeing. One is inside the other.

## DOUBLE MANIFESTATION

Manifestation is always double: the subject and the object—the subject, the

---

* *Nama* in Sanskrit means "mind," and *rupa* means "body."

cognizer; and the object, the cognized. So *vijñapti*, manifestation, is a double manifestation. Any manifestation is recognized as having its subject and object. In Chinese, there are two parts of the character for consciousness, one signifying the subject of cognition and the second indicating the object of cognition. But looking more deeply we see a third part, that serves as the base for the first two parts. Look at a coin. You have the head and the tail. The head is one part, the tail is one part, and they cannot be separated. The recognition that there are two faces of the coin is clear. But if you look deeply you see that there is a substance that makes possible the manifestation of the two faces and that is the metal, the substance, which is *svabhava* in Sanskrit. Every seed in our consciousness: the seed of joy, the seed of sorrow, the seed of fear, the seed of anger, the seed of mindfulness, the seed of concentration—every seed has within herself these three parts always together.

When I look at a mountain, I may think that it is an object that can exist apart from consciousness, which is the basic error. When you look at a cloud as an objective thing, as a reality out there, that doesn't have anything to do with your consciousness, that's the basic error. The cloud and mountain are just the object of your eye consciousness. And your consciousness, comprised of subject and object, is based on a foundation, for the manifestation to be possible. That is the third part, the substance.

## THE WAVE AND THE WATER

An example we often use in Buddhism is that of the wave and the water. The wave springs from the ocean and when you observe the phenomenon of the wave, you see there is a beginning and an end. You see the coming up and the going down, you see the presence and the non-presence of the wave. Before arising it seems that the wave did not exist, and after going down, we don't see it existing either. We distinguish between one wave and the another wave. One wave may be more beautiful, higher, or lower than the other wave. So concerning the world of phenomena we have all kinds of concepts: beginning, ending; high, low; more beautiful, less beautiful—and that creates a lot of suffering. But at the same time we know the wave is also water. It's possible for a wave to live her life as both a wave and water at the same time. As a wave, she belongs to the world of phenomena: she has a beginning, an ending, a coming up, a going down. She distinguishes herself from other waves. But if she has the time to sit down and to touch her nature deeply, she'll realize that she is water. She is not only a wave, she is also water. The moment she realizes she is water, she loses all her suffering. She's not afraid of going up and coming down anymore. She's not worried about being there or not being there anymore. Water represents the noumenal world, the world of no-birth and no-death, no coming and no going.

If you go a little bit deeper, you will see that what we do together, what we say together, what we think together will have an effect on us and on the world, now and later on. In the Buddhist teaching, nothing is strictly individual and nothing is strictly collective. These notions are relative.

You might think that your body is your individual possession, but your body belongs to the world as well. Suppose you are a driver and your safety depends on your optic nerve. You think of your optic nerves as something strictly individual; they belong to you and you are the one who profits from them and is responsible for them. But if you are a bus driver, all of us who sit in your bus rely on your optic nerves very much. Our lives depend on you. That is why to say, "It's my own life!" is a bit naive. We are in you and you are in us. We inter-are.

Seeing a flower, we identify it as a white rose, and we are very certain that it is an objective reality that exists separately from our consciousness—whether we are thinking about the flower or not, it is there. It belongs to the objective reality outside. That is the way we tend to think. But we have learned from science that the colors we perceive are a matter of the vibration of a particular wave of light. If the wavelength is too short or too long we don't perceive it. When frequencies are appropriate to our sense organs we believe that these things exist. But when we do not perceive the frequency, we think that they don't exist. I may ask another human being: "Do you see the same thing I see? Do you hear what I hear?" And that person says: "Yes, I do see what you see, I do hear what you hear." Then you have the impression since both of us agree, that it must be like that, that it is something objective and outside. But we forget the fact that we human beings are made in a similar way. Our sense organs are made in a similar way. We all agree that this is a table; we call it "table." We agree that it is a support for us to write something on. Because we are human beings we have the tendency to look at this as a table, as an instrument. But if we are born termites, we look at the table a different way. We may see it as a source of food, succulent, tasty, and nutritious. The termites are built in such a way that the table becomes food; we are built in such a way that the table is a support for our writing and reading. That is why what we believe to be the reality outside may only be a mental construction. Because our sense organs are built in such a way, we receive the so-called objective world in a certain way, and we believe that it's objective reality. We know that the rose is a collective mental construction of a group of living beings called humans. That is participation in a realm of being. The bees have their realm of being, the birds have their realm of being, the humans have their realm of being, and that realm of being is a collective manifestation, a collective conception of their karma, of their consciousness, their store consciousness.

In the Buddhist teaching, because mind is not local, it cannot die, it can only transform. You continue in the environment. Store consciousness, your thoughts, your speech, and your actions bring about the fruit of karma, which is comprised of yourself and your environment. You and your environment are one and create your karma. It is possible for us to assure a beautiful future by taking care of our thoughts, our speech, and our actions. You have the power of changing yourself within, and you have the power of changing yourself by changing your environment. Taking care of yourself means to take care of your body and to take care of your environment. It is not true that the genes determine everything. Through producing your thoughts, speech, and actions, you create your environment. You always have the opportunity to arrange yourself and arrange your environment in such a way as to water the positive seeds in yourself. That is the secret to happiness.

Of course our environment is not just made up of the things we see around us. There are things that we do not see or hear. And we tend to describe them as nonexisting. Suppose we look at the space in a meditation hall. The space around us is full of television, radio, and cell phone signals that we cannot see or hear. We need the mechanism—the phone or the television—to translate them for us. Often what we describe as emptiness is really quite full. It is our mind consciousness that translates all these things into sounds and colors. So I'm not sure that the leaf I held is inside or outside my mind. We have to be humble and open to allow the truth to penetrate. The secret of Buddhism is to remove all ideas, all concepts, in order for the truth to have a chance to penetrate, to reveal itself.

## OUR TANGLED MIND

The Buddha told an interesting story about a merchant who lived with his little son. And the mother of the little boy was no longer alive. So the little boy was very precious to him. He cherished the little boy, feeling that without him he could not survive—and we understand that. One day he was away on a business trip. The bandits came, they burned the village, they kidnapped the children, and they kidnapped the little boy. So when the father came home he was in despair. He was looking for his little son but he could not find him anywhere. In that state of extreme worry and despair he saw the dead body of a child, burned. And he took it to be his little son. He believed that his child was dead. In despair he threw himself to the ground, he beat his chest, he pulled his hair, and he reproached himself for having left the little boy alone at home. After having cried for a day and night, he stood up, he collected the dead body of the child, and he organized a cremation ceremony. Afterwards, he took the ashes and put them in a very beautiful velvet bag and he carried it with him all the time, because he loved the little boy so much. When you love something or someone so much, you want that something or someone to be with you all the time, twenty-four hours a day; and that we understand. Now because he believed the little boy was dead, and these were his very ashes, he wanted to carry those remains of his beloved one with him. Whether sleeping, eating, or working he always had that little bag with him.

One night at about two o'clock in the morning, the son, who had managed to escape, was able to go home. He knocked on his father's door. You can imagine the poor father was lying in bed, not able to sleep, still crying with the bag of ashes.

"Who is that knocking at my door?" he called.

"It's me, Daddy, it's your son."

The young father believed that this was someone trying to trick him, because he believed that his son was already dead. He said, "Go away, naughty kid. Don't disturb people at this time of the night. Go home. My son is dead." And the boy insisted, but he still refused to recognize that it was his own child who was knocking at the door. Finally the boy had to go away, and the father lost him forever.

Of course we know that the young father was not wise. He should have been able to recognize the voice of his own son. But because he was caught in a belief, and his mind was covered up by sorrow, despair, and conviction, he wasn't able to recognize that it was his own child knocking at the door. That is why he refused to open the door, and he lost his little boy forever.

Sometimes we take something to be the truth, the absolute truth. We are attached to it; we can no longer release it. And that is why we are stuck. Even when the truth comes in person knocking at our door, we refuse to open it. Our attachment to our views is one of the biggest obstacles to our own happiness.

Suppose you are climbing a ladder. If you come to the fourth rung and you believe that it is the highest, then there is no chance for you to climb to the fifth, which is truly higher. The only way that you can climb higher is to let go of the fourth.

One day, the Buddha came home from the woods with a handful of simsap leaves. He looked at his monks and he smiled, saying, "Dear friends, do you think that the leaves in my hand are as numerous as the leaves in the forest?" And of course the monks said, "Dear teacher, you hold just ten or twelve leaves, and in the forest there are millions and millions of them." And the Buddha said, "That's true, my friends, I have a lot of ideas, but I don't tell you. Because what you need is to work for your own transformation and healing. If I give you too many ideas, you get stuck in them, and then you have no chance to receive your own insights."

## THE THREE NATURES OF AWARENESS

So how do we perceive the world without these preconceived ideas? How do we look at the world with true awareness? There are three natures that describe how we perceive the world in varying degrees of awareness, *parikalpita*, *paratantra*, and *parinishpana*. The first nature is parikalpita, our collective mental construction. Our tendency is to believe in a solid, objective world. We see things as existing outside each other. You are outside of me, and I am outside of you. The sunshine is outside of the leaf, and the leaf is not the cloud. Things are outside of each other. That is the way most of us see things. But what we touch, see, and hear is only a collective mental construction. What most of us consider the nature of the world is only the nature of parikalpita. The person next to you says she sees and hears the same thing as you do. This is not because these things are the only, the objective, way to see the world, but rather because she is made very much like you and perceives very much the same thing.

We know that we don't see just with our eyes. Our eyes only receive the image that will be translated into the language of electrical signals. The sound we hear is also received and translated into electrical signals. Sound, image, touch, and smell are all translated into electrical signals that the mind can receive and process.

In the Diamond Sutra, the Buddha said, "All conditioned *dharmas* (things) are like a dream, are like magical things, are like water bubbles, are like mere images, are like a drop of dew, are like a flash of lightning...."* What we conceive to be personalities, people, what we conceive to be entities, dharmas, are just mental constructions, evolving in many ways, but they are all manifestations coming from consciousness.** Knowing that the world we live in is parikalpita, we look deeply into the world of mental construction and touch the second kind of perception, paratantra.

Paratantra means "leaning on each other, depending on each other in order to manifest." You cannot *be* by yourself alone, you have to *inter-be*

* Any phenomenon is a dharma.
** For more about this, see Thich Nhat Hanh, *Understanding Our Mind* (Berkeley, CA: Parallax Press, 2006).

with everything else. Looking into a leaf, you can see the cloud and the sunshine; the one contains the all. If we remove these elements from the leaf, there is no leaf left.

A flower can never be by itself alone. A flower relies on many non-flower elements in order to be able to manifest. If we look at the flower and see a separate entity, we are still in the realm of parikalpita. When we look at a person, like our father, our mother, our sister, our partner, and if we see them as a separate self, *atman,* then we are still in the world of parikalpita.

To discover the empty nature of people and things, you need the energy of mindfulness and concentration. You live your day mindfully. Anything you come in touch with, you look into it deeply, and you are not fooled anymore by its appearance. Looking into the son, you see the father, the mother, and the ancestors, and you see that the son is not a separate entity. You see yourself as a continuation—that is, you see everything in the light of interdependence and interbeing. Everything is basing on everything else in order to manifest. As you continue to practice, the notion of "one" and "many" will vanish.

The nuclear scientist David Bohm has said that an electron is not an entity in itself, but is made of all the other electrons. This is a manifestation of the nature of paratantra, the nature of interbeing. There are no separate entities, there are only manifestations that rely on each other to be possible. It's like the left and the right. The right is not a separate entity that can exist by itself alone. Without the left, the right cannot be. Everything is like that.

One day the Buddha told his beloved disciple Ananda, "Whoever sees interbeing, that person sees the Buddha." If we touch the nature of interdependence, we touch the Buddha. This is a process of training. During the day, while walking, sitting, eating, or cleaning, you can train yourself to see things as they are. Finally when the training is complete, the nature of *parinishpana,* reality, will reveal itself entirely, and what you touch is no longer a world of illusion, but the world of the thing in itself.

First, we become aware that the world in which we live in is being constructed by us, by our mind, collectively. Secondly we are aware that if we look deeply, if we know how to use mindfulness and concentration, we can begin to touch the nature of interbeing. And finally when the practice of awareness has gone deep, the true nature of absolute reality, stripped of notions, concepts, and ideas, even ideas of "interbeing" and "no-self," can be revealed.

Spiritual practitioners don't use sophisticated research instruments. They use their inner wisdom, their luminosity. Once we get rid of grasping, of notions and concepts, once we get rid of our fear and our anger, then we have a very bright instrument with which to experience reality as it is, reality free from all notions, notions of birth and death, being and nonbeing, coming and going, the same or different. The practice of mindfulness, concentration, and insight can purify our mind and make it into a powerful instrument with which we can look deeply into the nature of reality.

In Buddhism, we speak of pairs of opposites, like birth and death, coming and going, being and nonbeing, sameness and otherness. Suppose you have a lit candle and you blow out the flame. Then you light the candle again and you ask the flame this question, "My dear little flame, are you the same flame that manifested before or are you a totally different flame?" And she will say, "I am neither the same flame nor a different one." In teachings of the Buddha, that is called *madhyamaka,* the middle path or the middle way. The middle path is extremely important, because the middle path eliminates extremes, like being and nonbeing, birth and death, coming and going, same or different. And the findings of science already justify this kind of vision.

When you open the family album and you see a picture of the five-year-old child that you were, you see that you are quite different from the little boy or girl in the album. If the flame were to ask you, "Dear friend, are you the same as that little boy in the album?" you would answer just as the flame did, "Dear flame, I am not the same as that little boy, but I am not a totally different person either."

## USING THE MIND TO OBSERVE THE MIND

To have a vision of reality is one thing, but to put it into practice is quite another thing. Albert Einstein wrote: "A human is a part of this whole called by us 'universe,' a part limited in time and space. He experiences himself, his thoughts, and feelings as something separated from the rest, a kind of optical illusion of consciousness. This delusion is a kind of prison for us, restricting us to our personal desire and to a portion for a few persons nearest to us. Our task must be to force ourselves to free ourselves from this prison by widening our circle of compassion to embrace all living creatures and the whole of nature in its beauty."

Mind is not only brain. When you have a door to enter your house, you need a key to open the door. The key and the door are crucial for you to have access to the house. The manifestation of mind consciousness needs the brain, but that doesn't mean that the brain gives birth to mind consciousness, just as the door does not give birth to the house. The brain is not the only ground for the manifestation of consciousness.

In a retreat we create an environment where people can practice meditation: walking, sitting, breathing. Doing these practices gives them access to other dimensions of their minds. If, when we are too busy, we can talk of losing our mind, then, in mindfulness, we can find it again.

Many people are familiar with the story of the Sixth Patriarch of Zen Buddhism in China, Hui Neng. He lived at the Tung Chian Monastery of the Fifth Patriarch, Hung Jen. One day the Fifth Patriarch asked his monks to express their insight in a poem. His senior disciple, Shen Hsiu, had come from Northern China and was highly educated. He offered this *gatha:*

> The body is the bodhi tree.
> The mind is a great bright mirror.
> Every day you have to wipe it clean
> so that dust will not cover the mirror.

This poem is very good in terms of practice. Our mind tends to be clouded with craving, anger, fears, and worries. Our mind and the mind of our friends the scientists are of the same nature. Practitioners know how to take care of their mind, not allowing it to be covered up by layers of dust.

Hui Neng was from a peasant family in southern China. He had come north to study with the Fifth Patriarch. As he was illiterate, he had to ask one of his Dharma brothers to write out his insight gatha for him. The poem read:

> There's no such thing as the bodhi tree.
> There's no such a thing as the great bright mirror.
> From the beginning everything is empty.
> Where can the dust cling?

When observing the mind, you use the mind. And what kind of mind are you using to observe? If your mind is caught in anger, confusion, discrimination, then it's not clear enough to do the work of observation, even if you have expensive scientific instruments. The purpose of meditation practice is to help us have a clear mind to observe and help us untie the knots inside. Everyone has notions and ideas, and when we are stuck in them, we are not free, and we have no chance to touch the truth in life. The first obstacle is our concepts, our knowledge, our ideas about the truth. The second obstacle is *klesha*, our afflictions, like fear, anger, discrimination, despair, and arrogance. Walking, sitting, breathing, and listening to a Dharma talk are all ways to help sharpen the instrument of our mind so it can observe itself more clearly.

When you listen to a talk or read a book about the Dharma, it's not for the purpose of getting notions and ideas. In fact it's for releasing notions and ideas. You don't replace your old notions and ideas with new ones. The talk or the writings should be like the rain that can touch the seed of wisdom and freedom within you. That's why we have to learn how to listen. We listen or read not to receive more notions and concepts, but in order to get free from all notions and concepts. It's not important that you remember what was said, but that you are free.

We are used to working hard in school to remember things. We work hard to acquire a lot of words, notions, and concepts, and we think that this luggage is useful for our life. But in the light of the practice, it is a burden. So you are free from the burden of knowledge, notions, and concepts. You are free from the burden of afflictions, anger, and despair. That is why walking, sitting, smiling, and stopping is very important. Near the end of his life, the Buddha said, "In my forty-five years of teaching, I did not say anything."

When we eat our breakfast, eating breakfast becomes a practice. Looking into a piece of bread, even for a second or half a second, you can see the sunshine, you can see the cloud in the piece of bread. There is no bread without sunshine, without rain, without the earth. In the piece of bread, you see everything in the cosmos coming to you, to nourish you. That is deep awareness, deep mindfulness. And it's possible for you to deeply enjoy the piece of bread; it doesn't take a long time. A few milliseconds are enough for you to recognize that the piece of bread is an ambassador from the whole cosmos. When you put it into your mouth, you put only the piece of bread, not your projects, not your anger—it's not healthy to chew your anger or your projects—just chew the piece of bread, and enjoy chewing your bread. Only mindfulness allows us to live in such a way, deeply, touching the wonders of life, so that every moment can be a moment of healing, transformation, and nourishment.

## JUST ENJOY SITTING!

We can relearn how to sit, with the help of mind consciousness. Nelson Mandela, when he visited France, was asked by the press, "What would you like to do the most?" And he said, "Just sit down and do nothing. Since the time I was released from prison, I have been so busy—no time to sit and to just enjoy sitting."

To sit and do nothing does not seem to be very easy, because *vasana*, habit energy, in this case the habit of running, has become very strong—we feel we should always be doing something, and that has become a habit. That's why with the intervention of mind consciousness, with the insight that we can stop and begin to truly live our life, there is a possibility that we can enjoy sitting and doing nothing. Just enjoy sitting! Allow your body to be peaceful, to be solid, to be free.

Sitting in peace is an art. When you are sitting in peace, it is as if you are sitting on a lotus flower. When you are not sitting in peace, it's like sitting on glowing embers. So learn to sit as a Buddha. Some of us can sit like that already. Just enjoy sitting and doing nothing. It needs a little bit of training.

And let us learn how to walk—how to walk in such a way that we can enjoy every step, so that our projects, our fear will not remain an obstacle.

When we eat our breakfast, it's an occasion to sit, to eat, and enjoy every morsel of our breakfast. When we do our dishes, we can also be free, free from our projects and our worries, just enjoying washing the dishes. When you brush your teeth, enjoy brushing your teeth. While you put on your clothes, enjoy doing that. You are always with yourself, and you can enjoy every moment of your daily life.

# 4

## The River of Consciousness

T HE PHILOSOPHER David Hume said, "consciousness is a beam or a collection of different perceptions which succeed each other with an inconceivable speed."* Mental formations manifest and succeed each other like a river. When you look at the river you think that the river is one entity that remains very much the same. But that's a mental construction. As we sit on the riverbank we see that the river we're observing now is not the same river in which we just went swimming. Heraclitus said that you can never step into the same river twice.

In his book, *Evolution Créatrice*, published in 1908, Henri Bergson used the term "cinematographic mechanism of the mind" (*méchanisme cinématographique de la pensée*). When you look at a film you have the impression that a real story is happening. But if you hold up the strip of film and examine it, you see that there are only individual pictures succeeding each other and giving the impression that there is an entity, a continuum.

Mental formations manifest very quickly, succeed each other, and give the impression that consciousness is something long lasting. But if we are mindful and could look at one strip of film, we would see the life cycle of a mental formation and the nature of the seeds that create it.

We speak of seeds as having three natural characteristics and four conditions for manifestation. Each seed has its own characteristics that it maintains even though it's always changing. A grain of corn, although it's always changing, remains a grain of corn. When planted it will give you a plant of

* *A Treatise of Human Nature* (New York, NY: Oxford University Press, 2000).

corn, not a plant of beans. We can influence, modify, and transform a seed; it can acquire a better quality, but it maintains the same nature.

The first nature of the seed is that it dies in each moment to be reborn and die again. We know that the cells in our body undergo birth and death also. The flame at the tip of the candle also has the cinematographic nature. It dies in every split second to give rise to the next flame. Not only our consciousness, but also the object of our consciousness has the cinematographic nature. All things, whether physical or mental, are ever-changing. The Buddha said: "All formations are impermanent, dying in every kshana."

The second characteristic of the nature of a seed is that its manifestation, its fruit, is already contained in the seed. Suppose you have a DVD. You know it contains colors, pictures, and sounds; you don't see them and hear them, but you can't say they're not there. You need a few conditions to help them manifest. So the seed and the fruit are not two different things. It doesn't need time for the seed to become the fruit, because the fruit is already contained right in the seed. When you push the button to play the DVD, the sound, colors, and forms manifest right away. We don't have to wait until the seed grows into a plant for the plant to bring forth flowers and fruit. We don't need time; the fruit is already there at this moment in the seed.

The third characteristic of the seed is that it's waiting for different conditions in order to be able to manifest. The seeds are already there in our store consciousness, just as the signals and information on the DVD are ready. They're just waiting for certain conditions in order to be able to transform and manifest as sound, color, and form.

There are four necessary conditions for manifestation to take place. The first condition is seed condition, *hetu*. Without seeds, nothing is possible. Without information in the disk, you can't do anything. Without a grain of corn, no plant can sprout. If there were not seeds in store consciousness, it couldn't be called store consciousness, and the other seven consciousnesses which are born from it would not be able to manifest. Seed is the basic condition. With a seed of corn, we have the possibility of growing a cornstalk and having a few ears of corn to eat. The Chinese way of writing "seed" is very interesting. The word is made of two characters. One character means "limit," and inside it is the other character that means "big"—inside the limit is something that has the potential to become very big. The big already exists in the small. And if you allow other conditions to come in, that which is small will become big.

The second condition is the support for the seed. You have the seed of corn, but you need water, sunshine, soil, and the farmer to help the seed of corn to sprout and become a plant of corn. You have the seed of Buddhahood inside you. It's small. But if you give it a chance, it will bloom. You need conditions—you need a Sangha, you need Dharma brothers and sisters, Dharma teachers, a practice center. You need the kind of environment where the seed of Buddhahood can manifest to the maximum. These are supporting conditions.

Supporting conditions are of two kinds: in the same direction and in the opposing direction. If everything is smooth, it is in the same direction. But sometimes the conditions are of the nature to make the situation more difficult. Sometimes on your path, you encounter obstacles. Perhaps you have an illness, or you have a coworker who's very difficult to handle. But thanks to the difficulties, you can be transformed and you become much stronger. So that is a supporting condition as well, even though at first it seems like an obstacle.

There are pine trees that grow on very poor soil on the mountainside. There is very little nutrition there for a seed to sprout and grow. But because of that difficulty, the pine tree has the chance to go deep into the soil and become very strong so the wind can't blow it down. If the pine encounters only easy conditions along the way, then its roots may not go as deeply and firmly into the earth, and when the strong winds come it may be blown over. Sometimes obstacles and difficulties help you to succeed.

If you have a coworker who is difficult, you can see him as a supporting condition, even if he feels like an obstacle. He is teaching you something about your own strength. A practitioner should be strong in order to accept both kinds of supporting causes: same direction or opposite direction.

The third condition necessary for seed manifestation is called object as condition, *alambana pratiyaya*. For cognition to take place, there must always be a subject and object that manifest together. There can't be subject without object. We know that consciousness is always consciousness of something. When you get angry, you get angry at someone or something. When you eat, you must be eating something. So the object is a condition for the manifestation. Cognition always includes the cognizer and the cognized. Perception includes the perceiver and the perceived. A pencil lying on the table has a right side and a left side. The right can't exist alone; it can only be there if the left is there.

The same is true with consciousness. We tend to believe that consciousness is just there, ready to recognize whatever object presents itself. But perception itself is a mental formation. Imagination is a mental formation. Anger is a mental formation. Every time a mental formation manifests, subject and object are born together.

The fourth and final condition is steadiness, non-interruption. The word for concentration, *samadhi,* means to maintain steadiness, without going up and down. The object of your concentration may be a cloud, a flower, or your anger. In the state of concentration, you're keeping your focus steady and even. But if it dies and sometime later it's born again, then it's not concentration. It has to be continuous and steady.

Suppose you're projecting a film, and suddenly it stops. The sound and progression of images also stop. If there's an interruption in the process of consciousness, it will not be able to continue. There must be a steady continuation for the process to be possible. Suppose you plant a seed of corn and a few days later you dig it up to see how far along it is. You interrupt the growing process. For the young corn plant to grow you have to allow it to continue day and night, uninterrupted. If you blow out the flame on the tip of the candle, it can't continue. Your transformation and healing is like that. If your physician gives you antibiotics and asks you to take them for a certain number of days in succession, but you take them for only a few days and then stop, and then you begin taking them again some days later, it doesn't work. It needs to be steady and continuous.

When these four conditions—the seed, supporting conditions, subject and object arising simultaneously, and concentration—are present, then mental formations arise.

## The Particular and the Universal

If everything is connected, what is this distinction between the universal and the particular?

Suppose mind consciousness is observing an elephant walking. During the time of observation, the object of mind consciousness may not be the elephant in and of itself. It may only be a mental construction of the elephant based on previous images of elephants that have been imprinted in store consciousness. Mind consciousness has then lost contact with the particular; now it is in touch with the universal.

Suppose we look at a flower, and we are really looking deeply at that flower and know that that particular flower is the object of our mind consciousness. We have the capacity of touching the particular, the reality of things. In Buddhism, we often call this *svalakshana,* or suchness. When our sense organs touch the particular, we are designed in such a way that we usually perceive the universal sign of the image rather than the particular. When we see red, the color of a wildflower, we have the strong tendency to see the universal "red" instead of the unique hue presented to us in terms of light waves and vibration. This is the same concerning humans, animals, plants, clouds—we tend to see everything in their universal nature. We are no longer touching the particular, the basic elements. Store is capable of touching the particular as is mind consciousness. But mostly what mind consciousness touches is the image of the particular made into universals.

## Five Universal Mental Formations

The five universal mental formations are also, each in their own way, quite physical. They remind us of the way consciousness is both physical and mental. Touch is the first, followed by attention, feeling, perception, and volition. These five mental formations can take place very quickly, and their intensity, their depth, varies in each level of consciousness.

## TOUCH

In Buddhism, touch, the first universal, is defined as an agent, an energy that can bring three things together: sense organ, object of perception, and sense consciousness. When the trio is complete, the conditions for cognition will be possible. Before touch, these things may exist apart from each other. An eye is here, a cloud is there, and eye consciousness, in the form of a seed, is in store consciousness. In fact, all three are seeds in store consciousness. Touch provokes a modification, a change in the organ of eye consciousness, for example. Touch makes an impression on the organ, and that impression can be mild or it can be strong. If the impression is strong, it will be more stimulating, and it will have more of a chance to gain access to a higher level of consciousness. Otherwise, it will be recognized simply as something unimportant and will fall into the life continuum right away.

If there is an impression that's not too important, then, in just one kshana there's a vibration of the life continuum, and after that the surface of the life continuum will remain calm. We continuously are recognizing impressions as important or not important, something as already-known or unknown. Whatever is already known as well as whatever is considered to be unimportant, will be classified right away, very quickly, and will have no chance to get access to the higher level of consciousness. That's why we say touch is of different kinds. Whether a real feeling is obtained or not, depends on the intensity of touch. On this lower level the brain tends not to allow the information to go to the higher level of consciousness. It tends to dissuade and to bring everything down and process it right on the level of store consciousness. Most of what we receive in terms of touch and attention are processed on this level.

## ATTENTION

When the intensity of touch is important enough, the second universal will manifest, attention, *manaskara*. Attention is an energy that has the function of leading and orienting the mind toward the object, provided that touch is not something too familiar, not something dull. It should be something unknown, strange, important in order to arouse attention. Attention is like the rudder of a boat. If there's no rudder, then the boat doesn't know where to go. So the mind is invited to go in the direction of the object. You're interested in it; that's attention. It's like a courtier who introduces a peasant to the king. A peasant comes to the palace to see the king, but once there, doesn't know where to find him. So a courtier says, "The king is in this direction; I will take you to him." So attention has the duty of orienting the mind in the direction of an object that may be interesting.

Once touch has occurred between sense object and sense organ followed by attention, there is the phenomenon of seeing, of recognizing, through one or more of the sense doors. Attention is born and there is seeing, and then receiving the signals. The sequence of events is: the vibration of life continuum, the arrest of the vibration, and the sense door opening up. Then there is the five sense organs operating. And then there is the seeing, darshana, receiving the signals, and transmitting the signals. Then in the next moment is investigating. This is the processing of the information. This all happens in a matter of micro-seconds. In the eighth kshana, there is an act of determining consciousness and if the object of cognition is interesting enough, is powerful enough, during the next five or seven kshanas there is a continued procession called impulsion. During the time of these five or seven kshanas, there will be liking, disliking, a decision to do it or not to do it. So the element of free will may have a chance to intervene here. Finally during the sixteenth and the seventeenth kshanas, if the object is powerful enough, then it will be processed and recognized.

## THE KING AND THE MANGOES:
## A STORY OF THE PROCESS OF PERCEPTION

If the vibration of touch created by the object of one's perception is extremely weak, then on the third kshana it will sink into bhavanga, into life continuum, not having a very great effect on the upper level of consciousness. If the vibration of touch is stronger, then the perception has the chance to reach the fully aware mind consciousness. That is the process of a cognition as described by practitioners in the old time.

In the compendium of the *Abhidharma* an interesting example is given. Bhavanga, the store consciousness, is the sleeping king. There is a king taking a nap. The queen and some ladies in waiting are sitting nearby, because the king may wake up at any time and may need something. At the door of the inner palace there is a man who guards the door; he's deaf. He has the power to open or close the door. Outside there is a man who has come to offer the king a basket of mangoes. When the man with the basket of mangoes knocks at the door, the king wakes up. That is the vibration of the life continuum. Then a lady in waiting looks at the deaf man, makes a sign, and gives him the order to open up the door. The deaf man opening up the door is the sense door opening. The man with the basket of mangoes enters and people see the mangoes and become aware that someone is bringing the mangoes for the king. Then one of the ladies in waiting receives the mangoes. The queen comes and selects two or three ripe ones and gives them to a lady in waiting to peel for the king. Then the mango is offered to the king. During the next five or seven kshanas, the king eats the mango and there is liking or disliking, attachment or nonattachment. He might decide to eat just a little, or he might decide to eat a lot, and so on. After that, the king recognizes that he has eaten the mangoes, the mangoes are good, it's good that a person has come to offer him a few mangoes, and he evaluates the quality of the mangoes. After that he goes back to sleep. That is the process of a thought, of a perception. And you see that in the old times practitioners were already aware that the mind works very swiftly and all these processes of cognition take place in only seven to seventeen kshanas, a very brief moment.

## APPROPRIATE AND INAPPROPRIATE ATTENTION

The word "attention" is translated from the word *manaskara* in Sanskrit, *manasiikara* in Pali. Manaskara draws our attention to the object. This is also our practice. In the Buddhist teaching, we distinguish two kinds of attention: appropriate attention and inappropriate attention. If you're going to build a city, a Sangha, or a practice center, you should be able to create the conditions for appropriate attention to happen all the time. When your mind is directed toward something important, spiritual, beautiful, and wholesome it benefits the whole of your being, the whole of your consciousness. If your mind is led to something unwholesome, like being drawn to a group of people who are addicted to drugs, that's not appropriate attention.

In Buddhism we are urged to practice appropriate attention, *yoniso manaskara*. For example, a sister invites the bell to sound. There is touch when your ear comes in contact with the sound, and that gives rise to ear consciousness. When you hear the bell, you are oriented toward the object, the sound of the bell, and then you say, "I listen, I listen, this wonderful sound brings me back to my true home." And because of the orientation of the mind toward a wholesome object, you water the beautiful seeds in you. You establish yourself in the here and the now, you touch the depth of your being, and you receive healing and peace—that is what we call yoniso manaskara, appropriate attention. If you know the practice, you arrange your house, your living room, your schedule in such a way that you have many opportunities for your mind to touch what is wholesome and positive. Many people program a bell of mindfulness in their computer so that every ten or fifteen minutes there's a bell of mindfulness, and they enjoy breathing and smiling and not getting lost in their work. That is the practice of yoniso manaskara, appropriate attention.

If your attention is drawn to a dangerous, unwholesome situation and you get involved in that, it's called *ayoniso manaskara*, inappropriate attention. We need to use our intelligence to organize our life and create an environment where there are things and people to help us get in touch with positive, nourishing things. For instance, in a practice center everything should have the function of helping you to go home to yourself and touch the wonders of life within and around you.

## FEELING

The third universal mental formation is feeling. Touch has the duty to bring the three elements together and to serve as the foundation for a feeling.

Feelings are of three kinds: pleasant, unpleasant, or neutral. Touch can bring about feeling right away, and feeling can help bring more attention.

There are pleasant feelings that can lead to more healing and transformation, and there are pleasant feelings that can destroy your body and your compassion. So feeling is the kind of energy that can bring pleasure, that can bring suffering, or that can bring simple awareness of what is there—we call this functional feeling.

## PERCEPTION

The fourth universal is perception, *samjña*. Perception helps us receive the sign of the object, the characteristics of the object. For instance, when you look at a mountain, perception helps you see the characteristics of the mountain as form and colors. A mountain is not a river. A mountain has the appearance, the form, of a mountain. And a river has the appearance, the form, of a river. The role of perception is to see the form, the characteristics of the object. The second role of perception is to attribute a name to that object. That name may already be there in store consciousness. If you see the Pyrenees for the second time and you have already heard the name "Pyrenees," then during perception the old image of the Pyrenees and the name "Pyrenees" that you have stocked in your store consciousness come up to serve as the base of your present cognition. That's why we say that to cognize is to recognize and to give it a name. That is the nature and the function of perception. But the Buddha warned us to beware! Everywhere there is a perception, there is a delusion. We are all victims of wrong perceptions. Think of the lover who is full of wrong perceptions.

## VOLITION

The fifth and the last of the universals is volition. Volition is the energy that pushes you to do something, to run after something or to run away from something. It's the kind of energy that results from perceptions and feelings, and gives rise to an intention, the volition to do something. In the first case, you want to do it. It may destroy you, and yet, you still want to do it.

You may know intellectually that if you do it, you will suffer a lot. And yet you want it. It depends on the strength you have in your store consciousness. If you have enough wisdom and enough determination, then naturally you will say, "No, I'm not going to do it" and you are free—this is something very appealing.

There are other things that are appealing but which aren't dangerous. For example, going out to help people. You're motivated by the desire to help, to serve, to reconcile. Maybe there will be some danger, you may even lose your life. But if you have a lot of compassion, if you have the insight that there is no birth and no death, you are no longer afraid and you go anyway. That kind of desire is wholesome. That is volition.

And then there are the things you don't want to do. You want to run away from something, you're afraid of it, you're determined not to do it. Even if it's a good thing to do, you don't want to do it. "Why bother myself with helping other people? They're all ungrateful." So it all depends on the amount of wisdom and compassion that are already in store consciousness. Our decision at any time depends largely on the decision that has been made on the level of store consciousness.

Then there are some things you do that have only a functional nature. You just do it. It's not very important but it belongs to the practical aspect of life. It's not awfully important but you have the intention to do it and you do it.

The five universals always function at all times and at all levels of consciousness. That is why they're called *citta sarvatraga*, "always associated with consciousness." They always operate together and they are the content of consciousness. The level of consciousness determines the intensity and depth of the mental formations.

## THE PARTICULAR MENTAL FORMATIONS

The universal mental formations work pretty much the same way in each person. In a sense they *are* consciousness. What differentiates each consciousness are the particular mental formations: intention, conviction, concentration, mindfulness, and insight. With these particular mental formations, awakening is possible. Intention and conviction can help bring you to mindfulness, and mindfulness always brings concentration. And if you are concentrated enough, you begin to see the suchness of things more clearly.

## INTENTION

The first particular mental formation is intention, *chanda*. Intention is the wish to do something, for example, the intention to see, the intention to hear, the intention to touch. Intention can also be our determination to be mindful and our understanding that we can create the conditions for the habit of mindfulness. Neuroscientists have found that there is visible brain activity about two-tenths of a second before the beginning of intention. We could call it pre-intention. Often we don't realize we had the intention to do something until we are already doing it.

In your work, for example, you may notice that there are people who need to stop from time to time. One of the ways people take a pause is to sit back and light up a cigarette. While smoking, they don't have to think about business, they just go on a break. Breathing in and out will give you more of a break than smoking, but it requires the intention of mindfulness. Some people even program their computers so that every quarter of an hour they hear the sound of a meditation bell and enjoy stopping, breathing in and out.

Next time you eat lunch, observe the way you eat. Let us bring mindfulness to shine on every movement we make during the time of eating. We may have the impression that we operate very much like a machine. Although there is an intention to pick up a piece of tofu, although there is the act of picking up the piece of tofu, putting it in the mouth and chewing, we do it naturally without making any cerebral effort. Our mother, our father, our teacher show us how to chew, how to use knife and fork. With education, with the teaching, with the practice, we offer our store consciousness our manners and they become automated as good habits. We can take our intention to eat mindfully and make it as much a habit, a product of store consciousness, as the way we use our silverware.

## CONVICTION

The second particular mental formation is conviction, *adhimoksa*. Conviction is the confirmation of something well-established. You recognize something, you know what it is, and you have no doubt anymore. When you see the table, you say, "This is a table, I'm sure it is a table." That's atimoksa. You are really sure that this is a table. But you might be wrong. And still you have conviction. You see a person. You have the conviction that he is an enemy, a terrorist. You have no doubt that this person is an enemy because of the way he looks and the way he acts. And that kind of conviction leads to action. You will help him, you will rescue him, or you will destroy him depending on your conviction. Conviction does not mean that you are right in your perception, yet you have the feeling of being sure.

When we look at a rose we have the conviction that *this* is a rose. That is a conviction, but it does not mean that your conviction is justified. And conviction tends to be the base of action. It has the function of dissipating doubt. In the list of mental formations, doubt has been classified as unwholesome. But to me doubt has to be classified in the group of indefinite mental formations because doubt is sometimes helpful. If you don't doubt, you have no chance to discover the suchness of what is. In Zen Buddhism, the greater your doubt, the greater will be your enlightenment. That is why doubt can be a good thing. If you are too sure, if you always have conviction, then you may be caught in your wrong perception for a long time.

## CONCENTRATION

Concentration, *samadhi*, is the second particular mental formation. When we listen to a bell, we can listen very deeply. With the practice, the quality of listening becomes deeper and deeper all the time. You are capable of inviting all the cells in your body to participate in the listening, not just your brain or your nerves. There is a community of cells and we are fully focused on that. The Buddha used the word *sarvakaya*, the totality of the body. This is the third particular mental formation, concentration.

In whatever you do with intention, you can invite all the cells to participate. And if you do this deeply, then each cell behaves like the whole body, each cell becomes the whole body. There is no longer any distinction between this cell and that cell; trillions of cells are behaving like one. That is concentration. Mindfulness carries within itself the energy of concentration. Of course you have concentration, but the power of your concentration is different from the power of concentration of another person. If you continue to practice, your energy of concentration becomes more and more powerful, just by listening to the bell. If you can invite all the cells to join you and you listen as an organism and not just with your intellect, the situation will become very different.

When we are very concentrated in meditation we don't hear, see, or smell anymore. The five sense consciousnesses stop, because the concentration of mind consciousness is very powerful, so it is operating alone. But in our daily life there are plenty of times when mind consciousness collaborates with the sense consciousnesses. Suppose you are in an exhibition and you are absorbed in a work of art—it's so interesting and so beautiful, so your mind consciousness is totally absorbed in it. People are talking behind you and around you, yet you don't hear. Your energy is pooled and focused in one direction.

But concentration, in and of itself, is not necessarily positive. If you concentrate on the object of your craving, you can go crazy. If you concentrate object of your anger, you can go crazy. But if you concentrate on the truth of nonself, of impermanence, then your concentration will have a liberating effect. That is why we have to distinguish between right concentration and false concentration.

## MINDFULNESS

Mindfulness is written in Chinese with the characters signifying "now" and "mind." The Sanskrit is *smrti*. The first meaning of smrti is "to remember." And practicing mindfulness is remembering to remember. Mindfulness is the kind of energy that helps you to be aware of what is going on. When you are doing something good, you know, "I am doing something good." When you're doing something that you may regret later, you know: "I'm aware that I'm doing something I'll regret later." Mindfulness is in you. The seed of mindfulness is there, and whether it is still weak or has become powerful depends on your practice and your diligence.

We have to distinguish right from false mindfulness. It depends on the object of your mindfulness, and the way you handle mindfulness. If you only focus your attention on the negative things, the object of your craving, the object of your anger, and you lose your sovereignty, that is false mindfulness, that is negative mindfulness. The more you focus your mind on the person you hate, the more you hate him or her. Right mindfulness is to go back to your breathing in and out, and to become aware that anger is there, and that anger can make you suffer and make him suffer. That is right mindfulness: taking care of your anger and not focusing all your attention on the person you believe to be the source of your suffering. So we distinguish between right mindfulness and false mindfulness.

## INSIGHT

With concentration and mindfulness, the fifth particular, insight, is possible. Right insight, called *prajña*, has the power to liberate, to bring compassion and understanding. Wrong insight is a kind of affirmation that can be the opposite of the truth. You believe it to be the truth, you are so sure that it is the truth. You believe him to be the enemy. You believe that he is evil, so you have to destroy him if you want to have safety, security, and happiness. That kind of certitude is false insight. And many of us have false insight, wrong perceptions in us that are at the base of our actions, and our decision-making. That is why it is so important to distinguish between right insight and false insight. We have some ideas, and we are very sure of our ideas. If someone says, "Think again," it may help, and we may have a chance. To be too sure of something is very dangerous, especially when you hold a very important position in society and your decisions affect the lives of so many people.

For doctors, the wrong diagnoses can kill people, so they have to be careful. Doctors have told me that in medical school they are taught that even if you are sure, check again. This advice is doubly true for those of us who wish to practice mindfulness. Sometimes we are too sure of our perceptions. Our anger, our fear, our despair, our hate are born from our wrong perceptions. It would make you safer to write in calligraphy, "Are you sure?" and hang it in your office or workplace. That is a bell of mindfulness. Always go back to your perception, check it again, and don't be too sure of it.

# 5

## Perception and Reality

W ITHIN OUR STORE consciousness, we have direct access to reality, to suchness. At the root, the store, lies the basic wisdom in every one of us that has the capacity of directly touching reality in itself. Store consciousness has access to all the information that there is, to the totality of the seeds. But often, when we experience something with one of our senses, we have a preconditioned feeling of either attachment or aversion based on prior experience. We classify things according to the boxes we already have in our store consciousness.

Our perception of something tends to be based on the ground of our previous experiences. We've experienced something in the past and we compare it with what we encounter in the present moment and we feel that we recognize it. We paint the information with the colors we already have inside us. That's why most of the time we don't have direct access to reality.

There are oysters that live at the bottom of the ocean. A little bit of the light we enjoy up here is able to reach down there. But the oysters can't see the blue ocean. We human beings are walking on the planet. When we look up we see the constellations, the stars, the moon, the blue sky, and when we look down we see the blue ocean. We consider ourselves to be superior to the oysters, and we have the impression that we see everything and hear everything. But in fact, we are a kind of oyster. We have access only to a very limited zone of suchness.

Most of our inability to touch reality comes from self-ignorance, *atma avidya*. We can't see that the self is made only of nonself elements. Because we are attached to this idea of self, we end up with many complexes about ourselves, thinking we are superior, inferior, or exactly equal to someone else. We get caught in self-love, manas. That's how manas consciousness got the name "the lover," it's a lover with a lot of illusions that serve as the basis for attachment. This self-love makes it very difficult for us to perceive reality accurately. Think of how when you have a crush on someone, you don't really love him or her. You create an image and you love that image. That object of our love is not the thing in itself, it's not svalakshana. It's a mental representation of reality and not reality in itself. This is true whether we are looking at a mountain, at Paris, at a star, or at another person. Usually, we are just dealing with samanya, representations.

Manas lives in a realm of illusion. But mind consciousness and sense consciousness, like our store consciousness, have the capacity of touching reality in itself. This takes training, because many of us have lost that capacity. The good news is that, with the practice of mindfulness, we can restore our capacity for touching suchness.

Sense consciousness can often touch reality directly. Our eye, ear, nose, tongue, and body consciousness don't use inference or analysis. The direct mode of cognition is called pratyeksha pramana. When you look at a cloud, you don't have to think or reason. You don't have to use inference or deduction. You simply know.

Our mind consciousness can also touch reality through reasoning, anumana pramana. Our mind can use discursive reasoning, induction, deduction, and inference. Suppose from afar you see smoke rising. By inference you know that there's fire, because without fire there can't be smoke.

But direct perception is sometimes incorrect. Sometimes we are sure we heard something, a baby crying for example. But it is actually a cat. Because of our preconceptions, our sense consciousness can mislead us. Indirect perception, reasoning, is also often incorrect.

## Knowledge Is an Obstacle to Knowledge

Often it is our own knowledge that is the biggest obstacle to us touching suchness. That is why it's very important to learn how to release our own views. Knowledge is the obstacle to knowledge. If you are dogmatic in your way of thinking it is very difficult to receive new insights, to conceive of new theories and understandings about the world. The Buddha said to consider his teaching to be a raft helping you to the other shore. What you need is a raft to cross the river in order to go to the other shore. You don't need a raft to worship, to carry on your shoulders, and be proud that you are possessing the truth.

The Buddha said that even the Dharma has to be thrown away, not to mention the non-Dharma." Sometimes he went further. He said that his teaching is like a snake. It is dangerous. If you don't know how to handle it, you will get bitten by it.

One day in a meeting, a Zen master said: "Dear friends, I am allergic to the word 'Buddha.'" You know he is a Zen master because he talks about the Buddha like that. "Every time I am forced to utter the word 'Buddha' I have to go to the river and rinse my mouth three times." Many people were confused, because he was a Buddhist teacher. He was supposed to praise the Buddha. Fortunately there was one person in the crowd who understood. She stood up and said, "Dear teacher, every time I hear you pronouncing the word 'Buddha,' I have to go to the river and wash my ears three times." This is a Buddhist example of a good teacher and a good student!

## THE THREE REALMS OF PERCEPTION

The Buddha wrote:

> All composed things are like a dream,
> a phantom, a drop of dew, a flash of lightning.
> That is how to meditate on them.
> That is how to observe them.*

In Buddhism, we speak about three kinds of objects that we can perceive. The first kind of object is called the realm of reality in itself. It confirms that

---

* From the Diamond Sutra, see Thich Nhat Hanh, *The Diamond that Cuts through Illusion: Commentaries on the Prajñaparamita Diamond Sutra* (Berkeley, CA: Parallax Press, 1992) p. 25, 113.

our eyes, our ears, our nose have the capacity of reaching out to the thing in itself, even though we rarely operate in this realm in daily life.

The second realm is the realm of representations. Because of our attempt to grasp reality, reality is lost and we only receive the representation of reality, the world of representations. We have an idea of what the reality of someone is. We have an idea as to who she is and our idea is an idea and not the reality in itself. So we use notions, we use concepts in order to contain reality. When we look at a table we see the notion, the general universal "table-ness" of the table. Our perception of the table as a representation, however, does carry some substance of the thing in itself. It may carry some core of reality, but it is not reality in itself.

The third realm of objects of perception is mere image. When you dream, when you imagine, what you see, what you feel, belongs to the third realm, the realm of mere images, the images that are stored in store consciousness. You have seen an elephant, and the image of an elephant is stored down there in store consciousness. When you dream of an elephant, mind consciousness, which has access to store, goes down there and picks up the image of an elephant and the elephant you see is not the elephant of reality; it's not the elephant of representations, but the elephant of mere images.

These images, although not the thing itself, can be useful instruments for meditation. When we visualize something, that something is not really what we perceive with our sense organs. That something is the object or the outcome of our imagination. Suppose you visualize a Buddha. In a way, the Buddha in you is a mere image. But the mere image of the Buddha can help you to concentrate and help you to touch the real substantive Buddha, namely concentration, understanding, and compassion.

It is up to you to choose a Buddha and visualize him or her in you. If you can dwell with that image in concentration you can bring calm, joy, and compassion to your mind. There is a meditation that I learned as a novice monk that is useful to illustrate this point.

The meditation goes like this. First, you say to yourself, *The one who bows and the one who is bowed to are both by nature empty.* This means that I am in the Buddha and the Buddha is in me, so there is no separate self. That is the beginning of the visualization. You want to erase the difference, the duality between you and the Buddha. And you don't need an outside tool, an eraser, to erase the barrier between yourself and the Buddha. The mind is in itself a wonderful tool.

The visualization continues: *Our practice center is the net of Indra, reflecting all Buddhas everywhere.* Indra's net is described in Buddhist sutras as a net made of jewels, and in each jewel you see reflected all the other jewels. Looking into one you see the all. This means that all the Buddhas in the cosmos manifest in this practice center. You don't see one Buddha alone. You see countless Buddhas appearing.

Suppose you build a hall made of mirrors. Then you enter and hold a candle in your hand. Looking into a mirror you see you and the candle, and when you turn around you see you and a candle in that mirror, and you see you and the candle in another mirror reflected again. Not only does one mirror reflect another mirror, but it reflects all the other mirrors, because each mirror has you in it and the candle in it. You just need to look into one mirror and you see all the reflections of you and the candle to infinity. There are countless mirrors and countless candles and countless yous.

So when you get in touch with the Buddha and visualize the Buddha, you will find not just one, but countless Buddhas appearing around you. You visualize that in front of each Buddha there is one you who is practicing touching the earth before the Buddha. You cannot count the number of Buddhas and you cannot count the number of you. There is no limit. You also erase the idea that you are a reality and Buddha is another reality. You touch the nature of interbeing and you can release the notions of one and many, the same and different.

That is quite a difficult practice. It is more difficult than simply bowing to a Buddha statue or touching the earth in revererence. This is the practice of interbeing, and it begins with an image. So when we say that the realm of perception is the realm of "mere" image, do not underestimate it. It takes many years of practice. At the moment when you can do it, you feel wonderful. You can get rid of the notion of a separate self with this kind of practice. The practice of visualization is very important in Buddhism.

## THE MOTHER OF THE BUDDHA

In the Avatamsaka Sutra there is a very wonderful portion of the sutra describing the young man Sudhana looking for the mother of the Buddha. The young Sudhana has gone to many teachers in order to learn. His teacher is the great Manjushri Bodhisattva who encouraged his disciple to go and learn from many people, not only the old teachers but also young teachers, not only Buddhist teachers but also non-Buddhist teachers. Then one day Sudhana heard that he should go and meet the mother of the Buddha, because he could learn a lot from her. He went in search of her, but he spent a lot of energy and was not able to find her. Someone told him that, "you don't have to go anywhere, you just sit down and practice mindful breathing and visualization and then she will come." He stopped searching, he sat down, and he practiced. Suddenly he saw from deep in the earth a lotus emerge with one thousand petals. And sitting on one of these petals he saw the mother of the Buddha, the lady Mahamaya. He bowed to her and suddenly he realized that he was sitting on a petal of the same lotus. Each petal became a whole lotus with one thousand petals. You see, the one contains the all.

The lotus had one thousand petals. Lady Mahamaya was sitting on one petal, and suddenly that petal become a whole lotus with one thousand petals. He saw himself, the young man, sitting on one petal and suddenly he saw that his petal had become a whole lotus with one thousand petals. He was so happy, he joined his palms and looked up. And a very nice conversation began between the mother of the Buddha and the young man Sudhana. Mahamaya said, "Young man, do you know something? The moment I conceived Siddhartha was a very wonderful moment. It was a kind of bliss that permeated my whole being. The presence of a Buddha within yourself is a wonderful thing. You cannot be happier than that. You know, young man, after Siddhartha came into my womb, countless bodhisattvas came from many directions and asked my permission to go in and pay a visit to my son. Countless bodhisattva friends of Siddhartha came to visit to make sure that their friend was comfortable in there. They all entered my womb, millions of them. And yet I had the impression that if there were more bodhisattvas who wanted to go in, there was still plenty of room for them. Young man, do you know something? I am the mother of all Buddhas in the past. I am the mother of all the Buddhas in the present. And I shall be the mother of all Buddhas in the future." And that is what she said. Beautiful. Very deep. And that is the work of visualization, to show you the nature of interbeing, to show you the truth that the one contains the all. The smallest atom can contain the whole cosmos.

Who is Mahamaya, the mother of the Buddha? Is she someone outside of you, or you yourself? All of us carry a Buddha in our womb. Mahamaya is the lady who is very aware of that. While she walks, while she sits, she is very careful because she knows that she carries a Buddha within. Everything she eats, everything she drinks, everything she does, every film she watches, she knows will have an effect on her child. The Buddha Shakyamuni has said, "You are a Buddha. There is a baby Buddha in each of you." Whether you are a lady or a gentleman you carrry within yourself a Buddha. And yet we are not as careful as Mahamaya in our way of eating, drinking, smoking, worrying, projecting, and so on. We are not a responsible mother of the Buddha. And like Mahamaya, there is plenty of room inside us, not only for one Buddha, but for countless Buddhas. We can declare, like Mahamaya, that we were the mother of all Buddhas in the past. We can be the mother of all Buddhas in the present. And shall we be able to be the mother of all Buddhas in the future?

Is Mahamaya an outside objective reality? Or is she in ourselves? If you visualize that you are the mother-to-be of the Buddha, all complexes will vanish. You can behave with the responsibility of a Buddha's mother, so that the Buddha in you has a chance to manifest for yourself, for the world. That is why visualization is a very important tool. It can help us erase all these wrong perceptions in us so that reality can reveal itself very clearly to us.

## REALMS OF PERCEPTION IN DREAMS AND CREATIVITY

In a dream, you are mostly in the realm of perception, of mere images. You aren't using your eyes, your ears, your nose, or your tongue. But in the dream you see, you hear, and you speak. You see friends; you see strange living beings. You may see a war, bombs falling. You can see people dying. You can even kiss, you can even make love, but there's no one, no reality, not even representations. And you believe the dream to be true, to be something very real, because you cry and you laugh and you have all kinds of reactions. Despair, hate, anger, all these mental formations happen during your dream, when you see things, you hear things, you perceive things.

But if we observe deeply, we see that sometimes the realm of representations and the realm of the reality intervene during the dream. If you sleep in a very hot room—I hope that your room is not too hot—you might be dreaming of going to a bakery. Or if it's too cold you might be dreaming that you are swimming in ice. So the image of swimming in ice doesn't come only from the realm of mere image, it also comes from the realm of reality.

If you sleep with someone else, and that someone else in his sleep puts his head or his hand over you, you might dream that a ghost is sitting on you and you try to liberate yourself from that ghost. So the image of a ghost has something to do with the body of the other person. In a dream you may see that you are having sexual intercourse and perhaps you are losing seminal fluid. You wake up and you see that you are losing seminal fluid.

The three realms of perception are connected. The realm of representations is born on the ground of the realm of reality and carries some of the substance in it. And the realm of mere image is born from the realm of representations and from the realm of reality, and it may also carry some of the substance.

In the realm of mere image there are two kinds of images: those with substance and those without substance. Suppose in your dream you see your friend whom you know very well talking to you. That is a mere image with substance. But in the dream you also see a person you have not known before and that person may be the combination of several elements taken from here and there. Suppose you see an elephant. That elephant in your dream is a reproduction of an elephant, an image. It is very much like the real image of the elephant you see when you are awake. But suppose you see an elephant that flies in the sky; that is a combination. You take something of this, you take something of that, and make a creation of your mind, using your liberty, your fantasy, an image from the realm of representation.

As an artist, a painter, a poet, or an architect, you need to have a lot of imagination. You use the realm of reality and the realm of representation to create something that didn't already exist. What you create depends very much on your visualization and imagination. If you are an architect, you do not just draw the things that have been done before. You have to imagine new forms of architecture. Mind consciousness has the capacity of creating, not only works of art, but the world in which we live.

## THE FOUR REFLECTIVE INQUIRIES

When you speak about Paris, you mentally create an image of Paris in your mind. But we can look more deeply into mere images and representations to touch the reality within them. To do this, we need to inquire more deeply into the nature of the names we give things. Buddhists use a practice called the four reflective inquiries, the four *paryesanah*. Inquiry means not using the function of mental creation, but allowing yourself to get in touch and to try to see how things truly are. If we look deeply and are not deceived by the names of the selves and entities, we discover the true nature of the selves and entities. When we look into the reality that carries the name, we should be able to see it as it is, and not imagine about it. We practice not to be influenced by the name, because when we are caught in the name we can't see reality.

When you hear the word "cloud," the sound "cloud" brings about an image, a sign, with a shape, with a color, and the sound "cloud" can also bring about some kind of feeling and thinking. It is said in the teaching that when the bodhisattva looks at a name, inquires about a name, she only sees the name: name as name only.

In the Milindapañha, the king Milinda asks the monk Nagasana, "Is the consciousness of the babe in the womb, the same consciousness as that of the person who died?"* The consciousness of someone who dies is called

* See I. B. Horner, *Milinda's Question* (London: Pali Text Society); or online at accesstoinsight.org/tipitaka.

*kuskuti* consciousness. The consciousness of the one who is born is called *pratisamni* consciousness. Are these the same consciousness or different? The question of sameness and otherness arises. Is he the same person as the one who died before or is he a different person? That is the question put forth by the king Milinda. And Nagasana said, "Please think of yourself when you were three months old, a very tender baby. Are you the same as that baby? You will say, no, I'm now very big, very powerful, very robust, I'm not the same. But are you a different person, is your consciousness different? No, I am not a different person, because without that baby I couldn't be the king now." So the answer is that these are not the same, are not two different entities. And the answer given by the Buddha is, "Not caught in the idea of sameness, and not caught in the idea of otherness." You have the same name as when you were born, but only the name remains the same. You evolve all your life, so you have become different. Birth and death take place at every moment. So we look at reality without the nature of sameness and otherness and if we understand rebirth in that way, we are in the line of Buddhist thinking.

There is the story of someone who brings a pot of milk to her neighbor, and says, "Please keep this milk for me. I will go away for an hour and I will come back." But she was gone for many days, and when she came back, it had become yogurt. And she said, "No, no, it's not mine. I asked you to keep my milk but now you give me yogurt." So that person does not see the truth. The milk and the yogurt are not the same but they are not entirely different entities.

## THE FIRST REFLECTIVE INQUIRY: THE NAME

The first inquiry is on the name or the word, *nama paryesana*. We reflect on the name and on the word because they can evoke images, thoughts, and feelings. Each of us has a name. For most of us, our name hasn't changed, but we have changed a lot. So there's a gap between the name and the reality. We tend to believe that since the name remains the same, the reality has remained the same also. The name can be deceiving. When we hear the name we have the impression that we know the thing.

When you say "Christianity," you think that you know what Christianity is. You know the name and you think you also know the reality of Christianity. Hearing the name already brings about a feeling, a notion, an idea about Christianity. We have to be careful when we use a name. The reality that goes with the name may not be the reality of the thing in itself.

When we hear the word "Islam," we have ideas, feelings. Because we think we understand the name, we believe we understand Islam as a reality. But maybe our ideas about Islam are far from the truth. When someone describes a person to you, saying, "He is a Frenchman" the word "Frenchman" gives you an idea, a feeling right away. But it is only a name.

When we hear the word "terrorist," many of us immediately think of someone without a heart or feelings, who is evil and ready to kill us. There's a conviction that the terrorist is entirely another person; it could not be you. Yet when we look into the reality, we may realize that we are the one who creates terror inside of us and around us. But we still distinguish between the terrorist and the non-terrorist, and feel we belong to the camp of the non-terrorist. When we inquire into the truth, we see it differently.

A name can be very dangerous. To touch the nature of reality while inquiring into the word, we need to see that it is only a word and not be deceived by it. Names and words have a strong tendency to bring up feelings, emotions, and ideas of discrimination. With this awareness we will know how not to be caught in the word and in the name.

## THE SECOND REFLECTIVE INQUIRY: THE MEANING OF THE WORD

The second reflective inquiry is *vastu-paryesana,* to inquire about the meaning of the word spoken of in terms of selves and entities. Father, daughter, Buddha, Socrates, Saddam Hussein, Jacques, you, me, we are all called selves and each self bears a name.

In 1966, I was walking with other people in Philadelphia in a peace demonstration. A reporter came to me and asked the question, "Are you from the North or from the South?" North and South are names. That was a peace demonstration, an expression of the desire to stop the war in Vietnam. When I looked at him, I saw that in his mind he had two boxes of ideas and he wanted to put me in one of those two boxes. If I were to say I was from the North, then he would think I must be pro-communist and that my presence in the demonstration was to support communism. If I were to say that I was from the South, he would think this is someone who is anti-communist. As someone who has been in the practice of Zen meditation, I knew how dangerous it was to give an answer. Whether I answered North or South, it would only get him deeper in his notions and ideas. So I smiled and said, "I am from the Center." There is a region called Central Vietnam so I was telling the truth. That made him embarrassed, because he thought that there were only two choices—you must either be from the North or the South. Now he was lost. Because he was no longer sure of himself, he had a chance to inquire about the truth.

In the beginning of the war with Iraq, President Bush said, "Either you are with us, or you are with the terrorists."* It means very clearly that if you are not with us, you are our enemy and you should be destroyed. It means that there are only terrorists and anti-terrorists, and of course he believes he is on the side of the anti-terrorists. He feels that he has a noble mission to bring peace and civilization to the world. When you have such a conviction, this gives you a lot of energy. But we know that it's very dangerous to be caught in the words, to be too sure that we already know how things are. We're always ready to label things with the names and concepts that we already have.

## THE THIRD REFLECTIVE INQUIRY: CONVENTIONAL DESIGNATION

The third reflective inquiry is called *svabhava prajñapti paryesana*. Prajñapti means "conventional designation," which means that we agree with each

---

* George W. Bush in, "An Address to a Joint Session of Congress and the American People," September 20, 2001.

other to call something by a certain name. For example, a birth certificate is a conventional designation. We all agree that a birth certificate is a piece of paper that certifies that a child was born on a particular day. But looking deeply, we know that there is no birth, that the child is only the continuation of the father, the mother, the ancestors, the child is only a new beginning, a fresh start. Therefore "birth" is a conventional designation: we all agree about it, but we're not caught by the idea of birth.

If we sit and practice meditation together, we agree that over our heads is called the direction "above" and beneath us is called the direction "below." This is very useful. But as far as the truth is concerned, we should not be caught by notions of above and below, because our Japanese friends who are practicing zazen on the other side of the planet are sitting just as we are, but they wouldn't agree that our above is their above—it's really their below—and their above is our below.

Suppose we were to draw a stick. We would call one side of it the left and the other side the right. Suppose that you don't like the right and you wanted to get rid of it. So you cut off the right part, but when you do, another part of the stick becomes the right. Even if the distance between left and right is just a nanometer, there is a right side. Left and right are not realities, they are conventional designations.

If you are the son, you are not the father. But the son is only possible because the father is there. You think the son is something that is completely different from the father, that the son can exist outside the father. But that's not the case. And someday you're going to have a son of your own and you'll become a father. So son and father are just conventional designations, and they rely on each other in order to be. It's like three reeds that lean on each other in order to stand up. If you take one reed away, the other two fall down.

Selves and entities are all conventional designations. They're not real entities. They're not solid entities existing by themselves alone. So it's okay to call the Buddha "the Buddha." It's okay to call Osama bin Laden, "Osama bin Laden." But we should know that the Buddha is made only of non-Buddha elements, and that bin Laden is made only of non-bin Laden elements. The same thing is true with George W. Bush. If we look into President Bush, we have to see how President Bush has been made. We have to see the evangelical background, we have to see the geographical, cultural, and the religious background. If you haven't seen these things, you haven't seen Mr. Bush at all. Once you have understood how someone is made, then you understand that when we conventionally agree to call them a name or a title, like President, that is only a conventional designation.

This third level of inquiry brings us to the nature of interbeing. We can look and see that a flower is made only of non-flower elements. Another name for interbeing is interpenetration. Everything contains everything else; everything penetrates everything else. Looking into the one, you see the presence of the many, the presence of the all.

We're told that the human body is made of millions of cells. One cell contains all the cells, and carries within herself the totality of the genetic heritage. We can call it an individual cell but with the condition that we understand its interbeing nature. In other words, we have to see the term "individual cell" as a conventional designation.

The Buddha also speaks our language, and uses conventional designations. He spoke to his disciple Ananda, saying, "Ananda, would you like to climb the Gridhrakuta Mountain with me?" He used the words "you" and "me," and yet he was not caught. He knew that these terms are just conventional designations. The word 'nature," even the term "the interbeing nature," or "the nature of interconnectedness" is a conventional designation. We could call this "the non-nature nature," so we're not even caught in the idea that everything has the nature of interbeing, everything has the nature of interconnection, and we're not caught in the word "nature," in the so-called entity of "nature." That is why the Buddha had to go a step further and say "the non-nature nature." In the Buddhist literature we have the expression "no-nature," as the nature of everything. The word "nature" that we use in Buddhism is also a conventional designation. Because our mind tends to grasp things, it's important to receive teachings in such a way that we are not caught by them.

It's okay to use the name "Buddha," the name "nature," the word "you," and the word "me," if you have the insight of interbeing. We can call ourselves mother or father, son or daughter; we have to use these words. But when we use these words, we can remind ourselves that we are the father and, at the same time, we are the son.

## THE FOURTH REFLECTIVE INQUIRY: THE PARTICULAR

The fourth reflective inquiry is *vishesha prajñapti paryeshana*. Vishesha means "the particular." Svabhava means the universal, the general mark. Everything has a mark, an appearance. For example, when we look at flower, we see the general mark " flower." We see this in the realm of representation. But as we continue to look, we can see the particulars that have come together to allow the universal to manifest.

A house is an entity. When we look at a house, the universal mark "house" is perceived by us and we call it a house. But if we look deeply, we can see the elements of sand, cement, wood, glass, nails, and all the other things that have come together to make the house possible.

The universal is made of the particular. We may call a person Jack or Jill. But Jack is made of five elements: his body, feelings, perceptions, mental formations, and consciousness. And if we continue, we will see the many particulars that have come together to make the mark of the universal possible. The bodhisattva looks at the particular and recognizes that the particular is also a conventional designation, is not something separate and solid with an individual existence. While looking at the marks of the particular of a self or an entity the bodhisattva is not fooled by its mark. She realizes that not only in its universal mark is it a conventional designation, but in its particular marks it is also a collection of conventional designations. This practice is to help free us from grasping at names, selves, and entities, and help us touch the nature of paratantra, suchness, interbeing, so we can see the nishpana nature.

## NONDUALISM GIVES RISE TO NONVIOLENCE

Some neuroscientists tend to explain things in terms of monism, and see everything as interconnected parts of one reality. Others tend to explain things in terms of dualism. The question is frequently asked, "Are the brain and the mind one thing or two separate things?" Some believe that they are two separate things, and based on that dualistic view, they ask, "How can objective neural computations be transformed into subjective consciousness?" There are those who believe that mind and brain are one thing. Buddhist teaching guides us to look at things as neither the same nor different. This way of seeing things is something that can be experienced. When our father was born he was very small. As he grew up, he became bigger and changed in many ways. He hasn't been the same person throughout his life, but he's not two persons either. So looking into the reality, we see the truth of "neither the same nor different." You are his daughter, and you ask the question, "Am I one with my father, or am I a totally different person?" The teaching is clear, you are neither the same nor a different person from your father; you are a continuation. So dualistic thinking is misleading and can encourage a belief that good and evil are enemies and that good needs always to be fighting evil. This kind of theology causes a lot of suffering and destruction.

In the Buddhist teaching, anger has an organic nature. Love also has an organic nature. Suffering and happiness are also organic, and they inter-are. It's like garbage and flowers. A good organic gardener doesn't see the garbage as his enemy, because he has a clear perception of interbeing. He knows that he can use the garbage to make compost to enrich the soil, and the garbage can be transformed into flowers. He doesn't have a dualistic viewpoint. That is why he is at peace with the flower and at peace with the garbage. He knows that without the garbage he cannot have beautiful flowers.

When we know that our suffering, our hatred and fear are organic, we don't try to run away from them. We know that if we practice, we can transform them and they can nourish our happiness and well-being. Meditation is grounded in the insight of nonduality—nonduality between good and evil, suffering and happiness. So the method of handling our suffering is always nonviolent. When you accept the nondualistic nature of reality, your way becomes nonviolent. You don't feel the need to fight against your anger or your fear anymore, because you see that your anger and your fear are you. So you try to handle them in the most tender way. There's no fighting anymore. There's only the practice to transform and to take care. Anger and fear should be taken care of in the way that best gives them the chance to turn into love and compassion. In this way, the nondualistic foundation of meditation gives rise to the nonviolent way of practice. You handle your body and feelings in the most nonviolent way. If you're caught in the dualistic view, you'll suffer; you'll be angry at your body and your feelings. You're trying to run away, you're look for something that keeps you from being in touch with the suffering in your body or your emotions. But as we have learned, happiness cannot be without suffering, the left cannot be without the right—without this, that cannot cannot be.

To say that either you are with us or you are with the terrorists, shows that you are profoundly attached to the dualistic view. It's like saying "If you are not a Christian, you are against Christ." That's not sound theology. To say "if you're not with the Buddha, you're against the Buddha" is also not correct. In the teaching and the practice of Buddhism, we are always reminded that the Buddha was a living being and that there is no distinction between Buddha and living beings. If you remove the living being in the Buddha, he is no longer a Buddha. The essence of this teaching exists in all traditions.

"Either you are with us or with the terrorists" is not good politics. It's not good diplomacy either. Because the governments who don't hold the same view don't like to hear that. You alienate yourself from your allies when you say, "If you are not with us you are with the terrorists." No one likes to be with the terrorists.

We live in a time when meditation is no longer just an individual practice. We have to practice together as a community, as a nation, as a planet. If we really want peace to be possible, then we should try to look at reality in such a way that there is no separation. It's so important to train ourselves to look in a nondualistic way. We know from our own experience that if the other person is not happy, it's very difficult for us to be happy. The other person may be your daughter, your partner, your friend, your mother, your son, your father, or your neighbor. The other person may be the Christian community, the Jewish community, the Buddhist community, or the

Islamic community. Because we know that safety and peace aren't individual matters, we will naturally act for the collective good. Anything we do to help our friends, our neighbors, and other countries to be safer, to be respected, benefits us as well. Otherwise we are caught in our arrogance, and our dualistic view causes us to act in ways that will continue to destroy us and destroy the world.

## TWO VIOLET FLOWERS

We all know that the wonders of life are always there—the blue sky, the white cloud, the beautiful river, the rain, the flowers, the birds, the trees, the children. Yesterday during walking meditation I saw two little violet flowers in the grass. They were so beautiful, tiny, very well manifested, and I picked one and I picked the other, and I offered them to the two venerables who had come from Vietnam. I told them, "These flowers are available only in the Pure Land," and I am sure that the venerables understood the message. Because if we are mindful, if we can touch the wonders of life deeply, then the Pure Land, the Kingdom of God, is available to us. The fact is that the Pure Land is always available. The question remains, are we available to the Pure Land? To make ourselves available to the Pure Land is not difficult at all. Become mindful while you look, while you touch, while you touch the earth with your feet. It is possible for us to stay in the Pure Land twenty-four hours a day, with the condition that we keep mindfulness alive in us. There is a tendency to believe that this land is full of misery, suffering, and we want to go somewhere where there is no suffering.

My definition of the Pure Land or the Kingdom of God, is not a place where there is no suffering, because suffering and happiness inter-are. Happiness can only be recognized against the background of suffering. So we need suffering in order to recognize happiness. Looking deeply we know that happiness is not possible when we don't have understanding and compassion in us. A happy person is a person who has a lot of understanding and compassion. Without compassion and understanding you cannot relate to anyone, and you are totally isolated. Please observe and look around you and you will see that very well: the person who is full of understanding and compassion, that person does not suffer, he or she is happy. To be really happy, we should cultivate understanding and compassion. But if suffering is not there, it is impossible to cultivate understanding and compassion. It is by getting in touch with the suffering that understanding arises and compassion arises. Imagine a place where there is no suffering. Our children would have no chance to develop their understanding, to learn how to be compassionate.

It is by touching suffering that one learns to understand and to be compassionate. If in the Kingdom of God there is no suffering, there will be no understanding and compassion either, and without that you cannot call it the Kingdom of God or the Pure Land of the Buddha. This is something very clear, very simple. So my definition of the Pure Land of the Buddha, the Kingdom of God, is the place where there are plenty of opportunities for you to learn to be understanding and to be compassionate. When you have a lot of understanding and compassion, you are no longer afraid of suffering. It is like when you are a good organic gardener, you are no longer afraid of the garbage, because you know how to transform the garbage. That is the nondualistic way of seeing things. The little flowers I picked yesterday and offered to the venerables from Vietnam, are wonders. If we are not mindful, we cannot get in touch with them. The wonders of life are there, right in the present moment inside of us and around us. Our brain is a wonder. Our eyes are a wonder. Our heart is a wonder. Every cell of our body is a wonder. And around us everything is a wonder. All these things belong to the Kingdom of God, to the Pure Land of the Buddha. But we have lived in such a way that we totally ignore their presence. We get caught in our worries, in our despair, in our jealousy, in our fear, and we lose the Kingdom, we lose the Pure Land.

# 6

## Your Chance for Free Will

WHEN YOU WALK, you don't have to order your left foot to make a step; you don't command your right foot to make a step. It's not like that. You are just walking naturally, spontaneously, and if your mindfulness intervenes, it comes always a little bit later. That is why the question arises: Is our mind consciousness just a puppet of our store consciousness? If our mind consciousness is just a puppet, it would follow that the decision is made at the level of store consciousness where there is always implicit processing and implicit learning going on. Do we have free will or not?

Free will is possible, with the condition that you practice mindfulness. You use mindfulness and concentration to get insight. And with that insight you can make decisions based on the real suchness of things. You are not just a puppet of store consciousness. We have our sovereignty, but we have to use our sovereignty to water the positive seeds in store consciousness. Our future depends entirely on the value of our store consciousness.

### KARMA: YOUR THOUGHTS, SPEECH, AND BODILY ACTIONS

In Buddhism we also speak of store consciousness as retribution consciousness, *vipaka* in Sanskrit. Vipaka means ripening of the fruit. For instance, the nature of a fruit, like a plum, is the process of changing and ripening. In the beginning it is small, green, and sour. And if given the chance to grow, it becomes large, purple, sweet, and it bears a seed.

There is a tendency to imagine that we are an entity that is moving through space and time towards the future. We believe that right now we are ourselves and when we reach a point in the future we will still be ourselves. But that does not correspond to reality, because we are changing all the time. The Mississippi River has a name. The name Mississippi River remains the same, but the river is always changing, the water in it always changing. A human being is also like that. When we were born, we were a very tender baby of less than twelve pounds and now, as an adult, we are quite different in all aspects.

The human being is like a cloud. When we visualize ourselves as a cloud, we have an opportunity to look, to inquire deeply into the nature of a cloud. We may visualize how the cloud has been formed, how a cloud manifests itself. The word "cloud" can bring about the idea of this cloud or that cloud. This cloud is not that cloud. And the cloud is not the wind. The cloud is not the sunshine. The cloud is not the water.

Suppose part of the cloud has become the rain. And the cloud up there can look down and recognize herself as a stream of water. This is possible. When we see ourselves as a cloud, we can look around and see that we inter-are with other clouds. Other clouds will join us and we become a larger cloud. We begin to see more of the reality of the cloud; we begin to see more of the reality of the self. It is possible for a cloud to look down and to see that part of the cloud has gone ahead in other manifestations. It is possible for the cloud to smile to herself in the form of the stream of water on the surface of the Earth.

In each moment of our life, we receive input from the environment. We receive the air, we receive the food, we receive the image, the sound, and the collective energies. In every minute of our daily life, there is input. Every day we take in nutriments in terms of edible food, in terms of sensory impressions, in terms of thinking, in terms of education, and in terms of collective consciousness. And at the same time, we are putting out energy in terms of thinking, in terms of speaking, and in terms of acting. In every moment of your daily life, you produce thought, you produce speech, and you produce actions.

The French philosopher Jean Paul Sartre said, "We are the sum of our actions." Karma means action, and it can be expressed in terms of thought, speech, or bodily action. We are producing karma all the time and all of it goes in the direction of the future. That is why in our practice we should train ourselves to see ourselves in our actions, not only in this body. Of course, actions of body, speech, and mind also influence our body and feelings. When a cloud looks down, she can recognize herself as a stream of water. When we look down, we can see that we have gone into the future. We can recognize ourselves in many places.

You cannot say that when this body disintegrates, you are no longer there. You continue in many ways. When a cloud becomes the rain, the rain can be seen as countless drops of water. But when they come down to the Earth, they may join together into a stream again, or they become two streams or three streams, but that is the continuation.

## TRIPLE KARMA

Karma is of three varieties, that of thought, speech, and bodily action. To say that after the decomposition of the body nothing is left, is very unscientific. Antoine Laurent Lavoisier, the eighteenth century chemist, said, "Nothing is born, nothing can die." What will happen after your body disintegrates? The answer is that you are continued by your thoughts, your words, and your physical actions. If you want to know how you will be in the future, just look into these triple actions, and you'll know. You don't need to die in order to begin to see it—you can see it now—because in every moment you are producing yourself, you are producing the continuation of yourself. Every thought, every word, every act bears your signature—you can't escape. If you produce something not so beautiful you can't take it back—it has already gone out ahead into the future and begun to produce a chain of action and reaction. But you can always produce something different, something positive, and this new action of yours, in terms of thinking or speech or action, will modify the previous negative action.

When we go back to ourselves and we know what's going on, we have the power to shape our continuation. It is in the here and the now that we have the power to shape our continuation. Our continuation will not be something in the future. Our continuation takes place right here and right now. That is why you still have the sovereignty to determine your future. If you have done something good, you are glad. You say, "I can continue to produce more thought, more speech, more action of the same kind. Because I am assuring a good future for me and for my children." And if you have by chance produced something negative, you know that you are capable of producing things of the opposite nature in order to correct it, in order to transform it. Free will is possible in the here and the now.

Suppose yesterday I said something not very nice to my younger brother. That is something done, already done. It has created damage within me and within him. And today I wake up and I realize that I have produced a karma, an action that was destructive. Now I want to rectify that. I am determined that today when I meet him, I will say something different. From my insight, my compassion, my love, I utter a sentence. This sentence is produced now, not yesterday, but it will touch the sentence I said yesterday and transform it and correct it. Suddenly I feel healing taking place in me and healing taking place in my brother or my coworker, because this second act also bears my signature.

Suppose in the morning a person, full of impatience, yells at his child. This is a mistake, a negative action. And suppose in the evening, this same person does something very good, and he saves a dog from being run over by a car. That is a very good action. Each action is a seed planted in his store consciousness. No action, no thought, no word is lost. So where is that person going, if we combine action one and action two?

To know where you are going, in what direction, just look at the value of the seeds in your store consciousess and you will know your path. Everything depends on your karma, on your action, in terms of thinking, in terms of speaking, and in terms of acting. You decide, no one else decides your future. This is vipaka.

Every time you produce a thought, that's action. The Buddha proposed that we practice right thinking, thinking that goes in the direction of nondiscrimination, compassion, and understanding. We know that we are capable of producing such a thought, a thought of compassion, a thought of nondiscrimination. Every time we produce such a thought, it will have a good effect on our body and on the world. A good thought has the effect of healing your body, your mind, and the world. That is action. If you produce a thought of anger, hate, and despair that is not good for your health or the health of the world. Attention plays a very important role. Depending on the kind of environment you live in and what you pay attention to, you have a greater or lesser chance of producing good thoughts and going in the direction of right thinking.

Every thought that you produce bears your signature. You can't say it's not you. You are responsible for that thought and that thought is your continuation. Your thought is the essence of your being and your life, and once produced, it continues, it can never be lost. We can conceive of our thought as a kind of energy that will have a chain reaction in the world. That is why it's good to take care that we produce many good thoughts every day. We know that if we want, we can produce thoughts of compassion, understanding, brotherhood, and nondiscrimination and they each bear our signature, they are us, they are our future, they can never be lost. It is very clear that a thought of compassion, a thought of brotherhood, understanding, and love, has the power of healing: healing your body, healing your mind, and healing the world. Free will is possible, because you know that you can produce such a thought, with the help of the Buddha, with the help of your brother, your sister in the community, with the help of the Dharma that you have learned.

What you say also bears your signature and is your karma. Your speech may express understanding, love, and forgiveness. As soon as you use right speech, it has a healing effect. Right speech has the power of healing and transforming and can be used at any moment. You have the seed of compassion, understanding, and forgiveness in you. Allow them to manifest. You can stop reading right now and call someone and, using right speech, express compassion, empathy, love, and forgiveness. What are you waiting for? That is real action. Reconciliation can be obtained right away with the practice of loving speech. Right speech is in the direction of forgiveness, understanding, and compassion. Pick up the phone and do it. After you do it you will feel much better, the other person will feel much better, and reconciliation will occur right away. The thoughts you produced and the words that you have spoken will always be there as your continuation.

What can you do to relieve suffering? What kind of action can be taken every day to express compassion? Physical acts are the third aspect of your continuation. And we know that we are capable of doing something to protect people, to protect animals, to protect the environment. We can do something to save a living being today. It may be something small, such as opening a window for an insect to fly out of. Or it may be large, such as feeding or clothing someone who needs help. Each day we are in control of our karma, in little and big ways, and yet so often we feel as if we have no free will or control.

## NO BIRTH AND NO DEATH

You are responsible for the triple action (what you think, say, and do) that you produce in every minute of your life. The example of the image of a wave may be helpful. You see the manifestation of a wave, a young person with a lot of energy, a lot of hope, a lot of ambition, and that wave of youthfulness is moving up and up. And when you come to the crest of the wave you begin to go down. And when you go down, you also produce a kind of force. This is a force of two kinds. Force one is the karma energy, force two is the grasping energy. And when you go down as a wave, you also produce force one and force two. That energy is very dynamic, it is the ground of your manifestation in this form, and the manifestation of the environment in this form.

Looking at the level of the sea, you might think that the rising up of the wave is the beginning, the birth of the wave, and the falling down is the ending, the death of the wave. But if we consider the two forces, we know that this energy is not born from nothing. There should be a force that pushes the wave to rise up from the flat sea. And if there is a force before the so-called birth of the wave it means you had been there in the past. You are the continuation of another wave in the past, because there must have been a wave before you that is pushing very strongly and that is why you are born here. So the rising up of the wave is not really the wave's birthday, it is her continuation day. When the wave dissipates, it does not die. Nothing is lost.

Our understanding of continuation, though, doesn't contradict the basic Buddhist teaching of impermanence. If you believe that there is a soul that remains the same forever and ever, leaves a body and enters into another body through time and space, you are caught in the idea of a permanent self. The Buddha confirmed that nothing is lost, nothing can be annihilated, but he also said that nothing can remain the same forever.

When we inquire about the words "birth" and "death," we believe that there is a reality of birth beneath the appearance, a reality of death beneath the appearance. But if we are free from the word "birth," we have a chance to inquire about the reality of birth. In our mind there is a tendency to think that to be born really means that from nothing you suddenly become something, from no one you suddenly become someone. That is our common notion of birth. You didn't exist, and suddenly you exist.

Think of a sheet of paper, say the one these words are written on. The sheet of paper is supposed to have a birthday, like us—the day when it took this form in the paper mill. But paper is a word, it's a name, and the sheet of paper I hold in my hand is a reality. Before this sheet of paper took the form of a sheet of paper, it was still something. There were many things that came together in order to help the sheet of paper to take this form. We can see the trees, the forest. We can see the sunshine on the trees. We can see the rain on the trees. We can see the paste from which the paper has been made. We can see the worker in the factory. You cannot say this paper has come from nothing. Looking deeply, you see that the sheet of paper has never been born. The moment we call its birth is only a moment of continuation. Before that it had been something else.

So no one will die, just because no one has really been born. The moment of our conception in our mother's womb is not the moment when we begin to exist. We have existed before, in our mother, in our father, in our ancestors. We have not come from nothing. We are a continuation. It's like the stream of water on Earth is a continuation of the cloud in the sky. And the stream of water has not been born. It's only a continuation of the cloud.

When we hear the word "death," many of us are frightened because we think that death means the annihilation of the self. Death means from something you become nothing, from someone you become no one. But we are like the cloud and it's impossible for a cloud to die. A cloud may become rain or snow or ice or water. But it is impossible for a cloud to become nothing.

In our mind, to be born means that from nothing you suddenly become something; from no one you suddenly become someone. That is our definition of birth. But looking deeply, we don't see anything like that. A cloud has not come from nothing. A cloud has come from the lake, from the river, from the ocean, from the heat. A cloud is only the continuation of something. When a cloud dies, and you say the cloud "dies," you think it means from something you suddenly become nothing, from someone you suddenly become no one. But if you look deeply, you will see that it is impossible for a cloud to die. It's possible for the cloud to become rain or snow or ice, but you do not have the power to kill a cloud, to make the cloud into nothingness. The nature of the cloud is no-birth, no-death. The cloud will continue in other forms. It's not true that the cloud can become nothing. So when you hold the cup of tea and you drink mindfully, you recognize that the cloud that you contemplated yesterday in the sky—your beautiful cloud—is now in your cup, and you are drinking your cloud. You are touching the nature of no-birth and no-death of the cloud.

If someone you love just died, and if you are subject to a lot of grief, please use the insight of the Buddha. It's not possible for your loved one to die. If you use concentration, you will recognize him, you will recognize her in other forms. You don't see your beloved cloud in the sky, and so you cry. But your beloved cloud has become the rain falling joyfully on the ground and scolding you, "Darling, darling, don't you see me? I am here." Recognize your beloved cloud in her new form, the rain.

When you invite a bell a vibration travels through the air to reach you. Don't think that the sound of the bell has transmigrated from one place to another. There's an effect in terms of karma, a continuation. Everything you think, everything you say, everything you do has already begun to continue you. It is only a continuation; it's not a transfer of something from there to here. And we can make it possible for the continuation to be happy, to be pleasant. On our birthday we say, "Happy Continuation Day," rather than Happy Birthday, because every day is a continuation day. Through mindfulness, we can make sure that our continuation is good and beautiful.

## MOMENT TO MOMENT
## AND CYCLICAL IMPERMANENCE

Our continuation should not be confused with permanence. Even though the wave continues in other forms, each wave is also there for an instant and is gone.

Impermanence can be understood in two ways. The first is impermanence at every moment, "moment to moment impermanence." We have to see birth and death in every moment. And the other kind of impermanence is "cyclical impermanence." We see disintegration of the body every day. But underneath impermanence is continuation. Looking at the wave as a whole, you see the cyclical impermanence.

Returning to the cinematographic nature of consciousness, when you look at the film, you see the beginning and the ending of the film, and you see the cyclical impermanence. The film is no longer there, you see the words "The End." But the film is also made of separate moments, images that succeed each other and give the impression that this is an entity, a self. We can see both the cyclical impermanence and the moment to moment impermanence.

Karma, *vipaka*, can also be understood also in two ways: cyclical vipaka and moment to moment vipaka. Cyclical retribution takes our life as a whole and sees that the next life will be a retribution of this life. That is cyclical maturation. But vipaka is also taking place in every moment. This moment is the maturation of the moment that has come before it. Because what I have taught one minute ago already has had an impact on me and on you in this moment. It's like a candle that is in this very moment, in the here and the now, offering light, heat, and fragrance. And the light emitted by the candle illuminates the world outside, around, but also illuminates the candle. The light of the candle shines on the candle and shines on other things.

Similarly, we offer thought, speech, and action in each moment. What we think, what we say, what we do, has an effect on the world and has an effect on us. The world is us also, because we have gone out into the world right in the moment when we speak. We are projecting ourselves into the world all the time, and we are not only here, we are also there.

Anything you think, say, or do will have an effect around you and inside of you. You are not inside only, you are also outside your body. A good practitioner of meditation sees herself not only in this body, but also outside of the body. Can you see yourself outside of your body? If you do, you already have insight. You are not only continued inside, but outside. The triple karma energy is having an effect right here, right now.

As soon as you produce a thought, that thought has an effect on you right away. As soon as you produce a thought of compassion, of loving kindness, every cell in your body receives that wonderful energy, and if it is a thought of hate, of despair that you produce, right away it has a bad effect on every cell in your body and on your consciousness. Suppose you sign a check without money in the bank account. You don't see the effect now, but maybe one or two weeks later you will see very clearly. Or if a member of the Cabinet signs something or does something illegal, he might be able to hold his seat in the Cabinet and continue for a few years. But later on when they discover his corruption, he may be put in jail. So there are things that we do that will have an effect much later on. We distinguish two kinds of action: actions that come back to us very quickly in the here and the now and actions that will come back to us a little bit later on.

There is a line of poetry in Vietnamese that goes like this: "The non-body elements outside of the body are also the body, the nonself elements that you think are outside of the self, are yourself." You have to see your daughter as yourself, you have to see your son as yourself, you have to see what you have built, what you have destroyed as yourself, because all of them are the fruit of your actions, the triple action. That is how we should learn to look at ourselves. When you are able to see your continuation beyond this body, you begin to see yourself. What you term as the nonself elements outside of yourself, are yourself. You want to assure that the continuation of yourself will be beautiful. And this is something possible. If you are able to see the chain reactions of all these energies coming together, you won't say that after this point there will be nothing left. Because we know very well that nothing can be lost. Everything will continue.

When we are able to see what is happening in this present moment, we are also able to know what is happening in the moment we call death. There is a continuation, of course, but the continuation does not need to wait until the moment of death to be seen. The continuation is happening right here and right now. We are reborn in every moment.

## Mind Consciousness and Free Will

When mind consciousness operates alone it can be in concentration or in dispersion. Dispersion is when you allow yourself to be carried away by emotions. When we feel out of control of our lives, as if we don't have any sovereignty, that's mind consciousness in dispersion. You think and speak and do things that you cannot control. We don't want to be full of hate and anger and discrimination, but sometimes the habit energy feels so strong we don't know how to change it. There's no loving kindness, understanding, or compassion in your thinking, because you are less than your better self. Like the man who yelled at his child in the morning, you say things and do things that you wouldn't say or do if you were concentrated. You lose your sovereignty.

When we look deeply, we can already imagine ourselves in a situation in which we control ourselves better and we are not just the victims of our habit energies. Concentration gives us more freedom to make the choices we wish to make; it gives us the possibility of some free will.

When our energy is dispersed and we are angered easily, we may know, intellectually, that our anger doesn't help us, but we don't feel able to stop it. Thus the question of free will is not just an intellectual one. Sometimes people think that our feelings are only a matter of the chemicals that are released in our brain. You get angry, you get violent just because of some chemical substance released in your brain. But our ways of thinking and acting produce these chemicals. And the way they are released, over-released, or under-released depends very much on our way of life.

If we know how to eat in mindfulness, how to eat properly, how to drink properly, how to think properly, how to live our daily life in a balanced way, the release of these chemicals will only bring well-being. If we live a life that is disturbed by anger, fear, and hatred, then we know that at the base of our cognition the neurons and the chemicals they release will be affected, and there will be imbalance in the brain and in our consciousness. We can use our wisdom, our deep looking to determine how these elements function. You can't say these elements are not mind; they are our mind.

In Buddhism, we say this body *is* your consciousness. We use the Sanskrit expression, namarupa. "*Nama*" means mind. "*Rupa*" means body. They are not two separate entities, but a double manifestation of the same substance.

We know that all of us have negative habit energies that push us to think, to say, and to do things that intellectually we know will bring damage. And yet we do them anyway. We say them anyway. We think them anyway. That is habit energy. When habit energy comes up, and is about to push you to think, to feel, to say, and to do, you have the opportunity to practice mindfulness. "Hello there, my habit energy, I know you are coming up." That can already make a difference. You know that you don't want to be victim of your habit energy and the intervention of mindfulness can change the landscape.

The second thing mind consciousness can do is to learn positive habits. You can train yourself so that every time you hear a bell, you stop. You stop your thinking, you stop doing things, and you are supported by other members of the community to do that. In a few weeks it becomes a habit. When you hear the bell, naturally you stop thinking and you enjoy breathing in and out. That is a positive habit. The fact that we can create and cultivate a positive habit energy proves that free will is possible. Sovereignty over oneself is possible to some extent. Store consciousness and the habit energy in it are the ground for your daily thoughts, actions, and speech. You think, you speak, and you do things with store consciousness behind you dictating your behavior. The quality of the seeds within store consciousness is very important for that. You have some amount of wisdom, of compassion in you, and you still have an amount of anger, an amount of discrimination in you. Together with our education, with our practice, we can recognize that there is a mechanism existing on the unconscious level that causes you to walk, to sit down, to stand up, to think, to say things, and to act.

When mind consciousness begins to operate, the energy of mindfulness can be generated, and suddenly you are capable of being aware of what is going on. The intention to walk, the intention to make a step, may originate on the metabolic level. But it is possible to be aware of that intention. "Breathing in, I know that I have the intention to breathe in," even before you do it. Yet with the intervention of mindfulness, the landscape changes. Once intention has begun, mindfulness can still alter the course, and not by fighting. Mindfulness makes it possible for other seeds in us, positive seeds, to manifest. We have allies down in our store consciousness.

Mindfulness is the inviter. Mindfulness is the gardener who believes in the capacity of the soil to provide flowers and fruits. Sometimes mindfulness can play the role of the initiator. Suppose you are mindful that your beloved one is sitting in front of you. Breathing in, I know that my beloved one is sitting in front of me. And I notice that is something important. She is alive. She is present in front of me. It would be good if I say something nice to her, because tomorrow I may not be there to say it. And then you look at her, and you say, "Darling, I know you are there, and I am so happy." So, mindfulness can act as an agent and initiate some thought, or some speech, or some action. That is why we can say that mindfulness may come later, or mindfulness sometimes, if we want, can be the initiator of some thought, some speech, or some action. Understanding this process, we know there is a chance for us to be free. And great freedom begins with these little tiny freedoms that we bring about with our mindfulness.

## RECLAIMING YOUR SOVEREIGNTY

To me, mindfulness is our first real chance for freedom, for free will. In a state of dispersion, our mind is not together with our body. Our body may be here, but our mind is in the past, in the future, caught up in our anger, in our anxiety, in our projects. Mind and body are not together. So with mindful breathing we bring mind back to body. In English, we call it pulling oneself together. Pulling oneself together means that you become your better self. You recover some sovereignty of yourself. And you know that when you are able to bring yourself back together, there is some amount of mindfulness and concentration there. You are fully established in the here and now and you are aware of what is going on. You are no longer a victim of the situation, the situation of your body, the situation of your store consciousness, the situation of your environment. That is why mindfulness is so important. It can help us to be aware of what is going on. It can help us to initiate something. It can help us to recover, to reclaim our sovereignty.

With mindfulness we stop being the victim of habit energy. It's not that we fight the habit energy within us, rather, we become aware of it and embrace it gently. With the practice of mindful breathing, we become aware that habit energy is arising. We can say to ourselves, "Oh my dear habit energy, you are a long-time friend of mine. I know you too well. I will take good care of you." With that kind of mindfulness, you retain your freedom. You are no longer a victim of your habit energy. You know how to make use of many conditions in order to make your mindfulness stronger. A community that practices mindfulness, the sound of the bell, and the practice of walking meditation are all supportive elements.

With mind consciousness, and the practice of mindfulness, we can bring the past back to the present. We are still established in the present moment, we are not losing ourselves in the past, but we can bring the past back to the present moment for a look, for an observation, for a study. Established in mindfulness, you can pass in review the things that happened in the past, "Every time I did that, I got this or I got this." You can observe the law of cause and effect. In this way, mind consciousness is capable of learning from the past. Learning from the past will give us freedom, and that is an element to help us to make good decisions, decisions that will help us not to suffer in the present moment or in the future. Mind consciousness can help us learn about the past and also learn about the future, because the future is available here and now. We know that the future will be made only of the present moment. The substance with which the future is made is the present moment. That is why looking deeply in the present we already see the future. If there is peace, harmony, right effort, and mindfulness now, we know the future will be good. But if in the present moment we are only a victim of our habit energies, we know that the future will not be as good. We can already see the future now. That is how mindfulness can uncover not only the present moment, but also it can uncover the past and uncover the future.

There may be someone who has difficulty being himself. Whenever he's in a meeting, if he's provoked, he explodes. But one day someone comes and says to him, "Try once more. And this time you may succeed." But he refuses to try because he knows from experience that every time he sits in a meeting he explodes; he thinks he is just made like that. But the friend says, "Well, I will be with you, and that will make a difference. I will be holding your hand. And when you feel me pressing your hand, go back to your mindful breathing and don't say anything." So the friend trains him first. Then they both come to the meeting. During the whole meeting, the friend holds his hand. At the moment when the situation happens, he squeezes the hand of the other person. The other person already knows the practice of mindful breathing, so he practices breathing in and out and he refrains from saying anything. Perhaps for the first time in his life, this person does not explode in the meeting because there is a new element of mindfulness entering his life.

The supportive friend has been practicing loving kindness, he sees your suffering, and he brings his support to you. The friend is a condition of awakening, a condition for change. The Buddha, the bodhisattvas, and all those who practice compassion and understanding always try to provide people with the conditions to help them, so they can intervene in our life. Sometimes you yourself and sometimes a friend will bring the conditions for your awakening to you. Change comes from within and from outside, but change does come, giving each of us a chance for free will.

## INDIVIDUAL AND COLLECTIVE KARMA

Each of us has this chance for free will, but we cannot have it alone. Our individual karma, our environment, and our collective karma are interdependent. Earlier, we used the example of a candle offering light. The candle not only offers light, but it also offers heat, fragrance, and even water and carbon. This is the offering of the candle to the environment. The candle partly creates its own environment. And what the candle has created also influences the candle. The light emitted by the candle is shed back on the candle; you can see the candle very clearly by its own light. And the heat causes the wax to melt so that absorption of the fuel becomes easier. So everything the candle offers, the candle also receives.

Suppose there is a second candle and this candle also shines around herself. We may think of the first candle's light as individual, but you know that her light is also reaching the second candle. So the candle's light is not exactly individual and it is also not exactly collective. It depends on degree: more individual or more collective. There is nothing completely individual and there is nothing completely collective. The part is there in the whole and the whole contains the part. The light from the candles is a collective manifestation. It is the outcome, not of one candle, but of two candles. Imagine one thousand candles operating at the same time, and the light is a collective offering, a collective manifestation of all the candles.

When you come to Plum Village, the mindfulness community where I live, you offer your personal, individual energy. The way you think, the content of your thinking, the way you speak, the content of your speech, the way you act and the content of your acts all contribute to the atmosphere of Plum Village. If your thinking is compassionate and tolerant, you make a positive contribution to the beauty, the peace, the love of Plum Village. And if your thinking is full of discrimination, worries, and hate, you do not make a positive contribution. That is why everything is collective and personal at the same time. The collective is made of the personal, *and* the personal is made of the collective.

You think of your eyes as belonging only to you. But this isn't true in the light of collective manifestation. Remember the example of the bus driver.

It seems that the bus driver's optic nerve is his own property, but the lives of the passengers also depend on it. The collective and the individual inter-are. That is why karma can also be seen in terms of collective manifestation.

Retribution is in part individual, based on your thoughts, actions, and words. But it is also collective and in the environment. Looking at the forest you are aware that the trees are providing oxygen for you, and then you see yourself as the forest, as the trees, because without them you can't breathe. You see that the trees and the forest are part of your body. And in big cities you always have a central park. The central park in the city is our lungs, the collective lungs of everyone, of every citizen, otherwise we wouldn't have enough oxygen to breathe. We see it's very crucial that we have a park. That park is our lungs outside of this body.

I know there is a heart inside, and if my heart inside doesn't function, I will die right away. Therefore, I try to do everything I can to protect and to preserve my heart. But when I look at the red sun, and breathe in and out, I see that the sun is another heart of mine. If the sun stops operating I will die right away. That is why I consider the sun as my heart.* When you practice like this, you see yourself not limited by the skin of your body. You see that the environment is you. That is why the second aspect of retribution is environment. Taking good care of the environment is taking care of yourself.

The Diamond Sutra teaches us about the Four Notions. These are four misperceptions that we need to remove in order to see clearly. The first is the notion of self. That is not too difficult to understand, because we know self is made only of nonself elements. The second notion is a human being, and we know that humans are only made of non-human elements. The third notion is that of living beings. Usually we distinguish between living beings and the inanimate world, namely plants and the minerals. We know very well that if we pollute the minerals and if we kill the plants, then the animals have no ground on which to manifest and to continue. And if we pollute the mineral world plants have no chance to flourish as nourishment for the animal world. That is why such a vision helps you to see that your

* For more on this, see Thich Nhat Hanh, *The Sun My Heart* (Berkeley, CA: Parallax Press, 1988).

body is also the plants, your body is also the minerals, and to preserve the environment is to preserve yourself. The last notion we remove is that of life span. We are caught in the notion that we are here for eighty years, more or less, on this earth. That is a notion that doesn't correspond with reality. The insight of no-birth and no-death is the fuel that helps us to burn up the notion of life span.

Your environment is collective, but you yourself are also a collective manifestation. The lives of others depend heavily on your capacity of seeing the road clearly. Your life depends on others supporting the conditions for your livelihood. So your eyes are a collective manifestation, your mind is part of all our retribution.

In Plum Village, we use the logo of the lotus. There's a little temple in the lotus, and the three words *smrti* (mindfulness), *samadhi* (concentration), and *prajña* (insight) are around the ouside. Our practice is the practice of cultivating freedom. As mindfulness practitioners, you have to believe that freedom is possible. Our belief is not based on abstract ideas. We look around. We see that among our spiritual sisters and brothers, among our co-practitioners there are those who have acquired more freedom now than three years ago. Therefore our belief is based on direct experience and not just wishful thinking. If we look at ourselves, we see that we have a little more freedom now than we did yesterday.

Our practice is to bring mind and body together to be our better self. The quality of our being is determined by our energy of mindfulness, concentration, and insight. With that energy we can burn away a number of obstacles that used to bind us, or block our way. It can be said that the path of the Buddha is the path of freedom. Freedom, liberation, salvation are what we can observe in our daily life. Looking into ourselves, looking into the person of our sisters and brothers in the Dharma, we notice there is progress, there is a process of liberation going on, and we can support each other on that path of liberation. Our practice is not just for individual freedom, but collective freedom and liberation. We know it is possible.

# 7

## The Habit of Happiness

HOW CAN WE learn the practice of no-self? When you learn something for the first time, you use your mind consciousness to understand. And after some time it becomes a habit, and your mind consciousness doesn't have to be aware anymore. There's a process of forming habits, a tendency to automate everything and use our store consciousness, so that even if you don't pay attention to what you're doing, you can do it correctly, like walking. When you walk, your mind may be entirely absorbed in your thinking about other things, and yet eye consciousness collaborates with store consciousness enough for you to avoid accidents.

We use this process of turning information into store consciousness to create habits. If you operate too much with your mind consciousness, you get old very quickly. Your worries, your thinking, your planning, and your reflection require a lot of energy. A person named Wuzisi in ancient China spent just one night worrying and being fearful, and in the morning all his hair had turned white. Don't do that! Don't use your mind consciousness too much; it's consuming a lot of your energy. It's better to *be* than to think.

That doesn't mean we lose our mindfulness, rather our mindfulness becomes a habit that we can practice without forcing. Mind consciousness is the level at which we can train ourselves in the habit of mindfulness, and then it will infiltrate store consciousness, creating a pattern of mindfulness at the level of store. Mindfulness has the capacity to stimulate the brain, to engage with what we are perceiving in a new way, so that we are not just operating on autopilot. Is it possible to reprogram our store consciousness to respond with mindfulness rather than mindlessness? Is it possible to instill in our store consciousness the habit of happiness?

To do so, we have to learn the lesson of mindfulness with our bodies and with our store consciousness rather than with our mind consciousness. The lesson we're learning is that we have to treat our body as consciousness. The practice has to involve our body in it. You can't just practice with your mind, because your body is an aspect of your consciousness and your consciousness is a part of your body.

When our store consciousness and our sense consciousness (which we could also call our body consciousness) are in harmony, we will find it easier to cultivate the habit of happiness. When we're just beginning to practice, when we hear the bell we have to make an effort to concentrate, to enjoy the bell, to practice mindful breathing, and to calm ourselves. We use a lot of energy. But after practicing for six months, a year, or two years, it will happen naturally and the mind doesn't have to intervene. The bell goes directly to store consciousness through ear consciousness, and the response becomes natural. We don't have to make an effort anymore or use a lot of energy as we did in the beginning. That's how the practice can become a habit. When the practice has become a habit, we don't have to exert too much effort on the level of mind consciousness. This shows that good practice can transform old habits that are no longer serving us. Good practice can also create good habits. A time comes when we don't have to use mind consciousness to make decisions anymore—we just practice naturally. There are many of us who don't need to make a decision to practice mindful breathing. When we hear the bell, we practice mindful breathing naturally, and we enjoy it. So a behavior is less expensive once it's become a habit.

Mindfulness is a practice to enjoy, not to bring about more hardship in our life. The practice is not hard labor, it's a matter of enjoyment. And enjoyment can become a habit. Some of us only have the habit of suffering. Others among us have cultivated the habit of smiling and being happy. The capacity to be happy is the best thing we can cultivate. So please enjoy walking, enjoy sitting. We enjoy sitting and walking for ourselves, for our ancestors, for our parents, our friends, our beloved ones, and for our so-called enemies. Walking like a Buddha—that is our practice. We don't need to learn and understand all the sutras, all the Buddha's written teachings, in order to be able to walk like a Buddha. No. We don't need anything more than our two feet and our awareness. We can drink our tea mindfully, brush our teeth mindfully, we can breathe in mindfully, make a step mindfully. And it can be done with a lot of joy and without any fighting or any effort. It's a matter of enjoyment.

True happiness comes from mindfulness. Mindfulness helps us to recognize the many conditions of happiness that are available in the here and the now. Concentration helps us to get in touch more deeply with these conditions. With enough mindfulness and concentration, insight is born. With deep insight, we are free of wrong perceptions and we can maintain our freedom for a long time. With deep insight, we don't get angry anymore, we don't despair anymore, and we can enjoy each moment of life.

There are those of us who need a certain dose of suffering in order to be able to recognize happiness. When you have actually suffered, then you see that non-suffering is wonderful. But there are those of us who don't need to suffer and yet still have the capacity to know that not suffering is happiness, is wonderful. With mindfulness, we become aware of the suffering that's going on around us. There are many who can't sit like us, in calm and safety. A bomb or a rocket might fall on them at any moment, for example, in the Middle East or in Iraq. What they want is peace. What they want is the cessation of the killing. But they don't have it. There are many of us who have a chance to sit like this—in much more safety, many of us who live in a situation where this kind of suffering does not exist. But we don't seem to appreciate that.

Mindfulness helps us to be aware of what's going on around us, and suddenly we know how to treasure the conditions of peace and happiness that are available in the here and the now. We don't really need to go somewhere else in order to understand suffering. We need only to be mindful. You can stay wherever you are, and mindfulness helps you to touch the suffering of the world and to realize that many conditions of happiness exist for you. You can feel safe, happy, joyful, and powerful enough to change the situation around you.

The feeling of despair is the worst thing that can happen to a living being.

When you despair, you want to kill yourself or kill someone else to express your anger. There are so many people who are ready to die in order to punish others; they have suffered so much. How is it possible to offer them a drop of the nectar of compassion? How is it possible to make a drop of that nectar fall into their heart that is full of anger and despair? Each of us practicing mindfulness is able to get in touch, not only with the wonders of life that are nourishing and healing, but with the suffering as well, so that our heart is filled with compassion and we become an instrument of the bodhisattva Avalokiteshvara, the bodhisattva of compassion. It's always possible for us to be something, to do something, like Avalokita, to bring the nectar of compassion into a situation of despair.

## METHODS FOR CULTIVATING THE HABITS OF HAPPINESS

Based on what we have learned about the body and the mind, I'd like to offer the following exercises for cultivating concentration, mindfulness, and insight. These exercises are: the three concentrations, the six paramitas, Sangha building, and nondiscrimination. These teachings are at the heart of Buddhist practice and the secret to happiness. These teachings lean on each and support each other. If your concentration is powerful enough, you will make a discovery, you will get an insight. You need to be there, body and mind united, fully present—that is mindfulness. And if you are in that state of being, then it's possible for you to concentrate. If your concentration is powerful, you have a chance to make a breakthrough to happiness.

## THE THREE CONCENTRATIONS

There are three different kinds of concentrations. The first is emptiness. Emptiness here is a concentration and not a philosophy. Emptiness is not an attempt to describe reality. Emptiness is offered as an instrument. And we have to handle the notion of emptiness skillfully in order not to be caught in that notion. The notion of emptiness and the insight of emptiness are two different things. Let's consider a candle. In order to light up the candle, you light a match, you need the fire. And the match is only an instrument, a means. Without the match, you cannot produce the fire. Your ultimate aim is the flame and not the match. The Buddha offers you the notion of emptiness, because he has to use notions and words to communicate

Skillfully, with the use of the notion of emptiness, you can produce the insight of emptiness. Once the fire manifests, it will consume the match; when the insight of emptiness manifests, it will destroy the notion of emptiness. If you are skillful enough to make use of the notion of emptiness, then you have the insight of emptiness and you are free from the word "emptiness." I hope you can see the difference between emptiness as insight and emptiness as a notion.

Samadhi is not a doctrine, is not an attempt to describe the truth, but is a skillful means to help you to attain the truth. It's like the finger pointing to the moon. The moon is so beautiful. The finger is not the moon. If I point my finger and say, "Dear friend, this is the moon," and you catch this finger and say, "Oh this is the moon!"—you don't have the moon. You are caught in the finger; you cannot see the moon. The Dharma of the Buddha is the finger, not the moon.

The Heart Sutra says, "Form is emptiness, emptiness is form"—what does it mean? The bodhisattava Avalokiteshvara said everything is empty. And we want to ask him, "Mr. Bodhisattva, you say that everything is empty, but I want to ask you, 'empty of what?'" Because empty is always empty of something. That is a skillful way to destroy the word "emptiness" in order to get the insight of emptiness. Imagine a glass. We agree that it is empty. But it's important to ask the question that seems to be useless but is not, "Empty of what?" Empty of tea, perhaps. Empty means empty of something. It's like consciousness, perception, feeling. To feel means to feel something. To be conscious means to be conscious of something. To be mindful means to be mindful of something. The object is there at the same time as the subject. There cannot be mind without object of mind. This is very simple, very clear. So we agree that this glass is empty of tea. But we cannot say that this glass is empty of air. It's full of air.

When I observe a leaf, I see the leaf is full, totally full. I look at the leaf, I touch the leaf, and with the wonderful instrument called mind, I can see that while I touch the leaf I am also touching a cloud. The cloud is present in the leaf. I know very well that if there is no cloud, there is no rain, then no poplar tree can grow. That is why when I touch the leaf, I touch non-leaf elements. One of these non-leaf elements is the cloud. I touch the cloud; I touch the rain by touching the leaf. By touching the leaf I know that water, rain, cloud are there in the leaf. I also touch the sunshine in the leaf. I know that without the sunshine nothing can grow. I am touching the sun without getting burned. And I know that the sun is present in the leaf. If I continue my meditation I will see that I am touching the minerals in the soil, I am touching time, I am touching space, I am touching my own consciousness. The leaf is full of the cosmos—space, time, consciousness, water, soil, air, and everything, so how can we say it is empty?

It's true the leaf is full of everything, except one thing, and that one thing is a separate existence, a "self." A leaf cannot be by herself alone, a leaf has to inter-be with everything else in the cosmos. One thing has to rely on all the other things in order to manifest. One thing cannot be by herself alone. So emptiness is first of all empty of a separate self. Everything contains everything else. Looking into the leaf we see only the non-leaf elements. The Buddha is made only of non-Buddha elements. Buddhism is made only of non-Buddhism elements. And my self is made only of non-self elements.

## SIGNLESSNESS

The second concentration is signlessness, *animita*. Signlessness means not being caught by appearance. It looks as though the cloud that we observe in the sky has a beginning, and we speak of the "birth" of a cloud. It looks like a cloud may die sometime tonight and will no longer exist in the sky. We have a notion of birth and death. But with the practice of looking deeply, we can touch the nature of no-birth and no-death of the cloud. If we live our life mindfully, then we'll be able to touch the nature of signlessness. Drinking your tea, you recognize your beloved cloud is in your cup. The cloud may take the form of an ice cube. The cloud may take the form of the snow on the Pyrenees. The cloud may be in the ice cream that your child is eating. So with the wisdom of signlessness, you discover that nothing is born, nothing can die—and you have non-fear. True happiness, perfect happiness cannot be possible without non-fear. Looking deeply and touching the nature of no-birth and no-death will remove the fear in you.

There's the element of delusion in us and there's the element of luminosity in us. Because of the element of delusion, we suffer. Because of the element of luminosity, we can become a Buddha. That is how the duality between brain and mind can be solved. Reality is expressed as brain or as consciousness. It's not true to say that the brain is born from the mind, or the mind is an emergent property of the brain—you don't have to do that. You can say that both mind and brain manifest from the ground of store consciousness, and they support each other in their manifestation. Without mind, brain cannot be possible; without brain, mind cannot manifest. Everything relies on everything else in order to manifest. Like the leaf, like the flower—a flower has to rely on non-flower elements in order to manifest. The same thing is true with mind. The same thing is true with brain.

## AIMLESSNESS

The third concentration is aimlessness, *apranihita*. Without worry, without anxiety we are free to enjoy each moment of our lives. Not trying, not making great efforts, just being. What a joy! This seems to contradict our normal mode of operation. We are trying so hard to attain happiness, to struggle for peace. But perhaps our efforts, our struggles, our goals are the very obstacle to our attaining happiness, to our fostering peace. We have all had the experience of searching for an answer and then when we completely let go and relax the answer arises, effortlessly. That is aimlessness. We enjoy our breathing, drinking tea, smiling in mindfulness, walking in mindfulness and the insights come, the understanding shows up naturally. Aimlessness is a wonderful practice. It is so pleasant, so refreshing. I believe scientists need this practice as much as meditators, to unclench their minds, to open up to the possibilities that are beyond their imagination. Many scientific discoveries have happened on the ground of aimlessness, because when you are not set on your destination you have more opportunity to arrive at a new, unexpected insight.

## THE SIX PARAMITAS

The three concentrations can lead to insight. Another way to insight is through the six *paramitas*, six techniques for happiness. Paramita means that from this shore you go to the other shore. Happiness is there on the other shore. This shore may be the shore of fear, and it's possible for us to cross to the shore of non-fear. This shore may be the shore of jealousy and it's possible for us to cross over to the shore of nondiscrimination, of non-fear, of love. Sometimes we need only one second to go from the shore of suffering to the shore of well-being.

## GIVING

The first practice is the practice of giving, *dana paramita*. It is wonderful to give. When you are angry at someone, you have the tendency to punish him or her. You want to deprive him or her of this and of that; that is our natural tendency. But if you can bring yourself to give him or her something, your anger will vanish and you will go to the other shore right away, the shore of non-anger. Try it. Suppose from time to time, you get angry at your partner and you know that it will happen again in the future. So you go and buy or you make a gift and you hide it somewhere. Next time you get angry at him or her, don't do or say anything, just take the gift and give it to him. You will no longer be angry at him. That is the recommendation of the Buddha.

The Buddha taught us many ways to deal with our anger, and this is one of the ways. When you are very angry at someone, give him something, give her something, practice generosity. You don't need to be rich in order to practice giving. You don't have to go to the supermarket in order to make a gift. The way you look at him is already a gift. There is compassion in your eyes. The way you speak is a gift, because what you say is so sweet, is so liberating. A letter you write her can also be a gift. We are very wealthy in terms of thinking, in terms of speech, in terms of action; we can always be generous. Don't be thrifty. You can give at any time, and that will inspire the happiness of the people around you. Practice dana paramita. Always give, and you become richer and richer every moment. That is the first action of a bodhisattva, the practice of giving, generosity. Please remember that you don't need to be rich to practice giving.

## THE MINDFULNESS TRAININGS

The second practice is the practice of the mindfulness trainings, *shila paramita*. The practice of the mindfulness trainings is also a gift—a gift to you and a gift to the people you love. If you abide by the practice of the mindfulness trainings, you protect yourself, you make yourself beautiful, you make yourself wholesome, you make yourself safe, and that will support the happiness of the other person. By practicing the mindfulness trainings, you are protected by the energy of the Buddha, the Dharma, and the Sangha, you will not make mistakes anymore, you will not create suffering for yourself and for people around you. That is why the practice of the trainings is already a gift. The Five Mindfulness Trainings deal with integrity, honesty, and compassion.* They encompass protecting life, preventing war and destruction of life, practicing generosity, preventing sexual misconduct, practicing mindful, loving speech and deep listening, and practicing mindful consumption.

The practitioner of the mindfulness trainings has a powerful energy protecting him, protecting her, and preserving freedom and non-fear. If you practice the Five Mindfulness Trainings, you are no longer subjected to fear, because your mindfulness trainings body is pure. You are no longer afraid of anything. This is a gift to the whole society and not just to the people we love. A bodhisattva is someone who is always protected with the practice of the mindfulness trainings and who can offer so much from his or her practice of the mindfulness trainings.

* See Thich Nhat Hanh, *For a Future to Be Possible* (Berkeley, CA: Parallax Press, 1993, 2007).

## INCLUSIVENESS

The third technique to cross to the other shore is the practice of inclusiveness, *kshanti paramita*, the practice of helping your heart to grow larger and larger all the time. How can we help our hearts to grow every day, to be able to embrace everything? The Buddha gave a very beautiful example. Suppose you have a bowl of water and someone put a handful of salt in the bowl of water; it would be too salty for you to drink. But suppose someone threw a handful of salt into a clean mountain river. The river is deep and wide enough that you can still drink the water without tasting the salt.

When your heart is small, you suffer a lot. But when your heart becomes bigger, very big, then the same thing does not make you suffer anymore. So the secret is how to help your heart to grow. If your heart is small, you can't accept that person, you can't tolerate him or her with his or her shortcomings. But when your heart is big, you have a lot of understanding and compassion, and then there is no problem, you don't suffer, and you embrace him or her because your heart is so big.

We suffer because our heart is small. And we demand that the other person should change in order to be accepted by us. But when our heart is large, we don't put forth any conditions, we accept them as they are, and they have a chance to transform. The secret is how to grow our hearts. The practice of understanding helps the energy of compassion to arise. When compassion is there, we don't suffer anymore. We suffer because we don't have enough compassion. The moment when we have a lot of compassion, there is no suffering anymore. We encounter the same types of people, we encounter the same situations, but we don't suffer anymore because our love is so large.

Helping our heart to grow big, kshanti paramita, is the capacity of embracing everyone, everything, you don't exclude anyone. In true love, you don't discriminate anymore. Whatever a person's color, religion, or political beliefs, you accept them all with no discrimination whatsoever. Inclusiveness here means nondiscrimination. The practice of kshanti paramita has been understood as the practice of endurance. But the term endurance can be misleading. When you try to endure, you suffer. But when your heart is very big, you don't seem to suffer at all. Imagine that you have a basket of salt and you throw it into the river—the river doesn't suffer, because the river is so immense. People continue to draw water, to cook, and to drink, and it's okay. So you suffer only when your heart is small. That is why the bodhisattva can continue to smile. Practicing kshanti paramita, you don't have to suppress, to try to make an effort, because if you are suppressing, trying to bear it, it may be dangerous. If your heart is small and if you make too much of an effort, your heart might break. The practice of inclusiveness consists of helping our heart to grow bigger and bigger and bigger, and that is thanks to the practice of understanding and compassion.

## DILIGENCE

Diligence, the next paramita, is *virya paramita*. When we study consciousness in Buddhism, we understand the meaning of diligence in terms of store consciousness, in terms of seeds. In our store consciousness there are seeds of suffering and seeds of happiness, wholesome and unwholesome seeds. The practice of diligence consists of watering the wholesome seeds. It is a fourfold practice. First of all, arrange your life in a way that the bad seeds will have no chance to manifest. This takes a little bit of organization. We have to organize our life, our environment in such a way that the seed of violence, the seed of anger, the seed of despair in us has no chance to be watered. There are those of us who live in the kind of environment where negative seeds are watered every day. That is not diligence. We have to organize, we have to decide, we have to use our free will to organize our life, including our patterns of consumption. We know very well that there is a seed of despair, of violence, of anger, of fear in us. It's not healthy if we allow them to be watered and to manifest. If we live in the practice center, many things we hear and see help us to touch the wholesome aspects of our consciousness. Then the negative seeds have less chance to grow. You can discuss with others how to create the kind of environment, the way of life that supports you to prevent these negative seeds from being watered and manifesting.

And if by chance the negative seeds have been watered and manifest, what should you do? Arrange so that they can go back to their form of seeds as quickly as possible. And there are many ways for us to do that. Suppose by the practice of yoniso manaskara, appropriate attention, we pay attention to other objects of consciousness, interesting, peaceful, beautiful things. When we are in touch with the good things, then these unwholesome manifestations will go back to their original place as seeds. Among the methods prescribed by the Buddha is the method of changing the peg. In olden times, the carpenter used a wooden peg to connect two blocks of wood. He made a hole and drove a peg into the hole, securing the two blocks of wood together. If the peg rots, you can change the peg by driving a new peg into the same hole, so you replace the old peg with a new peg. That is an analogy for the technique of changing mental formations. When by chance the mental formation of anger is watered and manifests in your mind consciousness, you suffer, and now you try to use another mental formation to come and to replace it. In our time I wouldn't use the words "changing the peg," but "changing the CD." If the CD you're playing isn't good, you just stop it and put in another CD, because we have many beautiful CDs down in our store consciousness to choose from. So the second practice is to change the CD because if we allow the previous CD, or mental formation, to stay for a long, then that will continue to water the negative things and bring these things up again. So the second practice of diligence is to arrange it so that these negative manifestations will go back to being seeds as quickly as possible.

The third practice is to water the seeds that are wholesome and beautiful in your store consciousness, helping them to have a chance to manifest: the seed of compassion, the seed of love, the seed of hope, the seed of loving kindness, the seed of joy; you *do* have these seeds. So arrange your life and practice in such a way that these seeds can be watered several times a day in order for them to manifest. We can do that as a person, we can do that as a couple, we can do that as a Sangha, helping each other to water the wholesome seeds so that they can manifest on the screen of mind consciousness. When the wholesome seeds manifest, joy, freedom, and happiness become possible.

The fourth practice is to keep the positive seeds manifested as long as you can. It's like when you have pleasant guests visiting, you encourage them to stay as long as possible because they bring you a lot of joy. So keep the positive manifestations as long as possible. The longer they stay with us, the more opportunity we have for these seeds to develop at the lower level of our consciousness. As they are manifesting they serve as the rain to water the seeds of the same kind that are down there and they continue to grow and grow. It's like when you continue to watch violent television, the seed of violence continues to grow in you. If you continue to listen to Dharma talks, then the wholesome seeds of understanding and freedom in you continue to be watered. That is why diligence should be understood in the light of the teaching on consciousness.

## MEDITATION

The fifth technique is meditation, *dhyana paramita*. Meditation means to generate the energy of mindfulness and to maintain concentration. With mindfulness you can get in touch with the wonderful events of life for your nourishment and healing. Concentration helps you to look at everything deeply in order to discover the nature of impermanence, non-self, and interbeing. There are many kinds of concentration, including concentration of impermanence, concentration of no-self, concentration of emptiness, and concentration of interbeing.

## WISDOM

*Prajña paramita*, crossing over with the raft of wisdom, is the sixth paramita. We cultivate mindfulness, we cultivate concentration and understanding, and wisdom is the fruit of our cultivation. Wisdom is the fruit as well as the means to reach liberation. Liberation is found on the other shore. But it is not a matter of time, not a matter of distance to reach the other shore—it is a matter of insight, of realization. Releasing the shore of ignorance, of delusions, of attachment, of wrong perceptions, we are already touching the shore of freedom, of happiness. It is not a matter of time.

When you live deeply every moment with mindfulness and concentration your understanding, your insight always grows. It is our understanding that brings compassion, that liberates us from afflictions like fear, like anger. So a bodhisattva lives her life in such a way that the six elements of the practice grow every day. And from the shore of suffering, the shore of fearfulness, the bodhisattva can cross over to the shore of well-being and of non-fear very quickly. Because he has powerful instruments to do so.

As a Sangha, every one of us has the duty, has the joy to cultivate mindfulness. And our mind, our body, is the garden. When we touch the earth before the Buddha, before the bodhisattvas, we are encouraged to touch the Buddha within ourselves, the bodhisattvas within ourselves. We have to know that Avalokiteshvara, the bodhisattva of compassion, is not an entity outside of us. We have the capacity of being compassionate.

## FINDING WISE FRIENDS

One way to acquire this habit of happiness is to associate with wise beings. In the Sutra on Happiness, the Buddha tells us, "Not to be associated with the foolish ones, to live in the company of wise people, honoring those who are worth honoring—this is the greatest happiness."*

There are two kinds of wisdom. The Buddha speaks of the mind as luminous. When the luminous mind can't operate, it's because of the afflictions that are within us. If we can remove the afflictions, then the mind will operate as a mirror. When store consciousness is fully transformed, it becomes the Wisdom of the Great Perfect Mirror. It is direct, non-discursive wisdom, also called the "root wisdom," and it operates when we are able to remove afflictions like fear, ignorance, hatred, and craving.

When we study, do research and analysis, we are using the other kind of wisdom, called "later-acquired wisdom." This is the wisdom a philosopher or scientist uses to do analysis, reasoning, and inference. But innate within us is also the wisdom that can embrace and comprehend reality directly, not through discursive thought. You can surround yourself with people

---

* See Thich Nhat Hanh, *Two Treasures: Buddhist Teachings on Awakening and True Happiness* (Berkeley, CA: Parallax Press, 2007).

who cultivate that kind of wisdom, removing their ignorance, fear, and anger so that the Wisdom of the Great Perfect Mirror can be revealed. When hundreds of people around you do the same, a very powerful collective energy is born.

This collective community energy is called a Sangha. A Sangha means a community where harmony exists. If there's no harmony, happiness, brotherhood and sisterhood in the Sangha, then it's not a real Sangha. When real love and harmony exists, the Sangha becomes a living organism, and you are not there as an individual anymore, you are there as a cell of the Sangha body. When 300, 500, 1,000 people listen to the bell, the collective energy of mindfulness is very powerful and it will penetrate into the body and the mind of everyone.

To build a real Sangha, you need to know how to make use of the Buddhist practice of love. In the Buddhist tradition, the term "love" is translated as brotherhood or friendship, *maitri*. We translate maitri as loving kindness; it comes from the word *mitra*, which means friend. In a monastic community, we live together as brothers and sisters. When we love each other, we're not the possession of the other, we're not an object of consumption for the other person. Love has the substance of maitri inside, that is, the capacity to offer friendship and happiness.

Another element of true love is compassion, *karuna*, the kind of energy that helps remove suffering and transforms pain in the other person. When we're a Sangha practicing together, we're powerful, we don't become victims of our despair, and together we can live in such a way that we can be a positive factor for social change, bringing hope, and easing the pain of others. When you have the Sangha within your heart, the Sangha will be with you everywhere you go and anything you say will be what the Sangha wants to say to bring comfort, hope, and relief to the people around us.

I always feel wonderful sitting with the Sangha, practicing breathing in and out. That brings me enough happiness. Breathing in, I'm aware of the Sangha sitting with me, surrounding me. Your family is also a Sangha, a small Sangha. Your family may have only two, three, or four people, but you can very well transform it into a Sangha. If you know the practice, you can build beautiful Sanghas. It's possible to live happily in a community of one hundred, two hundred, three hundred people. If you don't have the practice, then two or three people can already make hell. But if you know the practice, then three hundred people can live together in harmony, happiness, and brotherhood. Sangha building is a very beautiful thing to do. And each member of the Sangha is a practitioner. She knows how to make peace inside and she knows how to help other members to make peace inside.

Finding a community that you respect to practice with is crucial to your happiness. This will help your store consciousness day and night, because store consciousness is both individual and collective. We're always receiving input from the collective consciousness. In receiving the positive input of the collective consciousness, the seeds of nondiscrimination, compassion, and joy in us will be watered every day. One of the most effective way to transform manas, our consciousness that is filled with attachments and illusions, is to be in the presence of a positive collective consciousness.

## THE FOUR ELEMENTS OF LOVE

When you are surrounded by others walking mindfully, it's much easier for you to walk mindfully as well. You allow yourself to be held, to be transported by the collective energy of the Sangha. And in the Sangha we are no longer a separate entity, we are no longer only individuals, we become a cell of the Sangha body. We are on the same frequency.

It's wonderful to be practicing in a Sangha with members who have deep experience in the practice, because when you see them and get in touch with them, you're inspired by the desire to do as they do. There are those of us who live very simply, who do not need to spend a lot of money, who eat simply, who have simple housing and transportation. And these people are truly happy, deeply happy. They are free enough to be happy, they are joyful enough, because their life has meaning. Every day they can be something, they can do something for the sake of others, including their brothers and sisters in the Dharma. Joy and happiness are possible, and we don't need a lot of money, fame, or power. Living mindfully, helping to build brotherhood, sisterhood, becoming a refuge for others, this brings you a lot of joy, a lot of happiness.

When we become aware of something and mindfulness is fully present, we can practice looking deeply into the object of our cognition and touch the nature of nonself, the nature of interbeing, the interdependence of everything. During that meditation, the element of insight is channeled to store consciousness. This is the rain of wisdom that will nourish the seeds of wisdom and compassion and weaken the seeds of self-complexes, self-love, and ignorance.

In many self-help books, self-love is considered a foundation of happiness. But in Buddhism, self-love is an expression of discrimination. "This is me and that is not me. I only take care of me. I don't need to take care of the non-me elements." When mindfulness intervenes in mind consciousness, the accompanying wisdom that is channeled into store consciousness already exists in store consciousness. You need only to water it and allow it to manifest. That is the wisdom of nondiscrimination, arising from the insight of interbeing, of nonself. Then it will be the wisdom of nondiscrimination that will be making decisions down there in store consciousness. And that will substitute for mentation. With the practice, mentation will be transformed little by little to become the wisdom of nondiscrimination. When the wisdom of nondiscrimination is present, the illusory image that manas has of store will disintegrate. There will no longer be any discrimination or attachment, and love becomes unlimited.

The four elements of true love are maitri (friendship), karuna (loving kindness), *mudita* (joy), and *upeksha* (equanimity). The last element, upeksha, is non-discrimination. Your love that is characterized by nondiscrimination is the love of a Buddha. Love that is still characterized by discrimination, will create suffering for you and for the other person. Cultivating nondiscrimination, upeksha, our love becomes true love, the love of the Buddha. With the practice, mentation is transformed little by little until it's replaced entirely by the wisdom of nondiscrimination, *nirvikalpajñana.* The lover becomes the true lover. We don't lose the lover. We replace the false lover with a true lover. And a true lover always has that quality of nondiscrimination, because a true lover has insight. She knows that the self is made of nonself elements, and in order to take care of the self, you have to take care of what is nonself. So instead of talking about self-love as the essence of happiness, we can talk about nonself as the key to happiness. That is the role of the practice.

# 8

# Walking with Buddha's Feet

O N THE OCCASION of my first visit to India I had the opportunity to climb the Gridhrakuta Mountain, just outside of Rajagriha, which was the capital of Magadha in the time of the Buddha. This was a mountain the Buddha used to climb to contemplate the sunset. I was reminded of this story. One day, Siddhartha was walking on the almsround in the city. This was before he became fully enlightened and became the Buddha. It happened that King Bimbisara was sitting on his royal cart and he saw that monk walking so beautifully, with dignity and freedom. He was a very polite person, though, so he did not stop the monk. After he went home to the palace, he gave an order to find out who that monk was. He was very impressed by the sight of Siddhartha walking as a monk in his own capital.

After a few days, his guards identified Siddhartha and where he lived. So King Bimbisara took a trip to the place where Siddhartha dwelled. He left his carriage at the foot of the hill and climbed up to see Siddhartha. During their conversation, King Bimbisara said, "It would be wonderful if you would accept to be my teacher. With your presence, the kingdom would be beautiful. And if you like, I would divide the kingdom into two and offer you half."

Siddhartha smiled and said, "Well, my father wanted to leave me a kingdom, but I did not accept. Now, why shall I accept half a kingdom here? My purpose is to practice to obtain freedom and to help people. I can't be the national teacher now because I have not reached full enlightenment. But I promise that when I get it, I will come back to you and help you." After that,

Siddhartha left the mountain. He knew that people were aware of his presence there. So the next morning he left the city of Rajagriha and went to the forest in the north to continue his practice and his journey towards enlightenment.

The Buddha remembered his promise to King Bimbisara, and a year after enlightenment, he came back to the city of Rajagriha to pay a visit to the king and share his teachings. But he was not alone now; he was accompanied by more than one thousand monks; the Buddha was a *quick* Sangha builder. In no time at all, he had nearly 1,200 monks following him.

He took care to train the monks properly in mindfulness before he brought them to the capital of Rajagriha. The monks learned how to walk, how to sit, how to stand, and how to go for the almsround in mindfulness. It is not easy to train more than one thousand monks to move around mindfully.

When the training was completed, they returned to Rajagriha. They stayed in a palm grove. The palm trees were still young, but it was a very beautiful palm grove. The thousand monks divided into groups of twenty or thirty and went into the city of Rajagriha for almsround. People were very impressed the first time they saw groups of monks walking mindfully, with dignity, with freedom, with joy. And very soon the news came to the king that Siddhartha was back. That day he brought many friends, ministers, and family members to the palm grove to pay the Buddha a visit. The Buddha gave them a wonderful Dharma talk and promised to pay a visit to the king in his own palace.

It took a fortnight for the king to prepare for the reception of the Sangha. On that day, everyone in the city knew that the king was receiving the monks. Thousands of people came to the street and welcomed them. There were moments when the Sangha could not advance because there were so many people on the street. There was a young gentleman, a singer, who appeared among the crowd and began to sing beautiful songs praising the Buddha, the Dharma, and the Sangha. It was really quite a festival and a beautiful day.

In olden times, the kings were always aware of the presence of a spiritual teacher within their kingdom and they would invite this teacher to beautify and sanctify the kingdom with their presence. That is why King Bimbisara tried everything in order to keep the Buddha in his kingdom. He wanted to own the Buddha and his Sangha. Politicians are like that. The first thing he did was to offer the Buddha and the Sangha a bamboo grove in the vicinity of the capital. The Bamboo Grove was large enough to house the 1,250 monks and the Buddha.

The king also gave the Buddha the Gridhrakuta Mountain. In the first years the Buddha was there, the only path up the mountain was a natural one, through the brush. But later on, King Bimbisara ordered a path to be built with stones. And the stone path built by King Bimbisara is still there today. If you go to Rajagriha—the new name is Rajgir—you can enjoy climbing the mountain by that path. You can also still visit the Bamboo Grove, where the government has restored several varieties of ancient bamboo.

King Bimbisara used to come and visit the Buddha, and he always left his carriage at the foot of the mountain and climbed. It takes time to climb. I don't know whether the king had learned walking meditation or not. The first time I climbed the Gridhrakuta Mountain I was accompanied by a number of friends, including Maha Ghosananda.* I was practicing mindful walking and enjoying every step I made, because I was aware that this is the path where the Buddha had walked. He climbed up and down the path thousands of times. Every day, he used the path. So, we were very mindful. We enjoyed deeply, because we knew that the footprints of the Buddha were there. We climbed about twenty steps and then we sat down and enjoyed our breathing and looking around, and then we stood up and climbed another twenty steps. Since I was accompanied by a group of people, at each stop like that I would give a three-minute Dharma talk, and after that, we resumed climbing, so when we came to the top we were not tired at all, not in the least. We felt the energy of the Buddha very strongly while climbing the path and while sitting on the peak of the Gridhrakuta Mountain. That day we practiced sitting on the peak of the mountain and contemplating the sunset. I was aware that the Buddha had sat like that

* Maha Ghosananda was the Buddhist patriarch of Cambodia.

many times and that he also saw the beautiful sunset. I was using the Buddha eyes in order to enjoy the beautiful sunset. The Buddha eyes have become my eyes, and we looked at that beautiful sunset together.

If you have an opportunity to go there, I suggest that you go very early in the morning, four o'clock in the morning, and you may hire a policeman to go with you—it's safer, because it's dark and there are so many poor people. The policeman I asked did not hold anything in his hand, not even a stick. His weapon was his eyes, because he knew everyone in the vicinity. If he recognized a thief, the thief would end up in jail. We had to pay him a only little bit of money, and he stayed with us the whole day. After the sunset when it became dark we could go down safely with him accompanying us.

Imagine a whole day climbing and sitting on the top of the mountain. You may like to have sitting meditation and walking meditation up there. You may like to have mindful lunch there. There was no toilet, no restroom, so you have to use the natural restroom. And the first time that I used the restroom up there, I was aware that the Buddha had done the same thing.

## The Energy of Mindfulness

It is possible to walk with the feet of the Buddha. Our feet, empowered by the energy of mindfulness, become the feet of the Buddha. You can't say, "I can't walk with the feet of the Buddha, I don't have them." It's not true. Your feet are the Buddha's feet, and if you really want to use them, it's up to you. If you bring the energy of mindfulness into your feet, your feet become the Buddha's feet and you walk for him. And that does not need some kind of blind faith. This is so clear. If you are inhabited by the energy of mindfulness, you are acting like a Buddha, you are speaking like a Buddha, you are thinking like a Buddha. That is Buddhahood in you. That is something you can experience; it's not a theory.

The practice of peaceful sitting and the practice of peaceful walking is very basic in Plum Village. We learn to sit in such a way that peace is possible during the whole time of sitting. We learn to walk in such a way that during the whole time of walking there is peace. And we rely on our mindfulness, on our concentration to do so. We also profit from the collective energy of mindfulness of the Sangha in order to do so. If we succeed in one day, we may succeed another day and so on. We have to be determined to succeed in that practice.

During walking meditation, for instance, if we are caught by a thought, if we think of what we have to do when we go home, then we lose the walking, we lose the opportunity. We are walking with the Sangha, but we are not there. We are not able to establish ourselves in the here and the now, and therefore we cannot make a peaceful, happy step. Or if we are worried about something, if we are angry with someone, we are not capable of making peaceful steps and we lose everything.

We know that while walking, we may not be free. And walking is a practice that frees us. We should walk like a free person. Freedom makes it possible for peace, for happiness to be with us. We have to invest one hundred percent of ourselves into every step in order to become free. If while walking we are caught, and a feeling of anger, or worries, or thinking of the past, of the future, of the other place arises, then we are not free. We are not really walking with the Sangha, because we are elsewhere. That is a waste. Breathing in, we may be aware that: I'm not really here, and I will regret this later. I have the opportunity, but I am not touching the conditions of happiness that lie in the here and the now. Am I able to be free? Am I capable of being peace right here, right now? We ask the question. We challenge ourselves. Because if you are not free, if you can't be free now, then you may not be free later on. Therefore you have to be determined to be free right here and right now. Although the mental formation of worry, or anger comes up very strongly, we know deep in ourselves there is the seed of freedom, the seed of peace in us, and we must do something in order for the seed of peace and freedom to manifest. We are not only the worry, the anger in us, we are more than our worry, our anger. And each person has to find effective ways to get free.

## THE INSIGHTS OF IMPERMANENCE AND NO-SELF

When we gain insight, we are able to see the true nature of impermanence. Often, we try so hard to make things stable in our life that the idea of impermanence brings up anxiety. But if we look deeply at the nature of impermanence, we might actually find it very comforting.

When you make a step, you may visualize that your mother is taking that step with you. This is not something difficult because you know that your feet are a continuation of the feet of your mother. As we practice looking deeply, we see the presence of our mother in every cell of our body. Our body is also a continuation of our mother's body. When you make a step, you may say, "Mother, walk with me." And suddenly you feel your mother in you walking with you. You may notice that, during her lifetime, she did not have much chance to walk in the here and the now and to enjoy touching the earth like you. So suddenly compassion, love is born. And that is because you can see your mother walking with you—not as something imagined but as a reality. You can invite your father to walk with you. You may like to invite the people you love to walk with you in the here and the now. You can invite them and walk with them without them needing to be physically present. We continue our ancestors, our ancestors are fully present in every cell of our body, then when we take a peaceful step and we know that all of our ancestors are taking that step with us. Millions of feet are making the same movement. With video techniques you can create that kind of image. Thousands of feet are making a step together. And of course your mind can do that. Your mind can see thousands and millions of your ancestors' feet are making a step together with you. That practice, using visualization, will shatter the idea, the feeling, that you are a separate self. You walk, and yet they walk.

The Buddha has offered us many practices so that we can be ourselves. The insight of impermanence is one tool we have. The insight of no-self is another. After all, the person we are angry at may be our son, may be our daughter, may be our partner, and his or her happiness is our own happiness. If that person isn't happy, I can't be happy. I don't want to be unkind to him or to her. Therefore I should be peaceful, I should be happy, because by being angry I do not help myself, I do not help him or her. If I suffer, there is no way that he or she can be happy. He is not a separate self and I am not a separate self; we inter-are. When you use the tool of nonself, and you touch the nature of interbeing, suddenly you overcome your anger and you are able to make a peaceful and happy step.

## WALKING IN THE PURE LAND

If you are walking with Buddha's feet, you are walking in heaven, you are walking in the Pure Land with each step. The practice of Plum Village is to walk in the Pure Land of the Buddha every day. Every time you move, your foot touches the Pure Land of the Buddha. That is written in one of our daily chants: *Every step helps me to touch the Pure Land.* That is the practice. Another verse: *I vow to touch the Pure Land in every step I make.* These chants are no longer a prayer, but a guide, a reminder of practice. You can do it; you know that you can do it. With mindfulness, you become aware of your step, and you touch the Pure Land with all its wonders. Such a step generates freedom, joy, and healing. We all know that walking meditation is to enjoy walking in the Kingdom of God, in the Pure Land of the Buddha, and walking like that can transform, can heal, can generate a lot of love inside. We walk not only for ourselves, we walk for our parents, our ancestors, and for those who are suffering in the world. The Pure Land is something we bring along with us wherever we go—a portable Pure Land. That is the best thing you can offer to the people you encounter. Offer them nothing less than the Pure Land or the Kingdom of God. You are a bodhisattva, that's the kind of gift that's worth making to the people around you.

## HUMAN CONSCIOUSNESS

About 1,500,000 years ago, humans began to stand up on their feet and their hands were liberated. Once they liberated their hands, their brain began to grow very quickly. Buddha nature is inherent in early man, even though the Buddha appeared on Earth only 2,600 years ago. We learned from him that other Buddhas have appeared before him, like Buddha Dipankara and Buddha Kashyapa.

There is a race of human beings who are capable of generating the energy of mindfulness all day. And we belong to that race, "conscious homosapiens." We all belong to the family of the Buddha, because we are able to generate the energy of mindfulness that inhabits us twenty-four hours a day.

Buddhas are those creatures who live mindfully twenty-four hours a day. In the beginning, we become part-time Buddhas, and as we continue to practice we become full-time Buddhas. We learn not to discriminate because we understand that *everyone* has the seed of Buddha nature. Every non-Buddha has the Buddha nature. That is why we are free from racial discrimination. And our practice is to help the Buddha nature manifest in as many people as possible, because collective awakening is the only thing that can bring us out of this present difficult situation. After enlightenment the Buddha already knew that he had to share the practice with many others. Buddha means "the awakened one," the conscious one. During the forty-five years of his ministry, the Buddha always tried to help other people to wake up, to be mindful. He always taught that the path of mindfulness, concentration, and insight is the path of liberation, the path of happiness.

## SEVEN WONDERFUL STEPS

The tradition says that when the Buddha was born he took seven steps—he practiced walking meditation right away. Siddhartha began to walk as soon as he came out of his mother's womb. Seven is a sacred number, so we can interpret it as the Seven Factors of Enlightenment and so on. When we celebrate the birthday of the Buddha, the best way to celebrate it is to make seven steps, real steps. I always think it's wonderful to be here, present on this planet and to make steps. It's the most wonderful thing to do. You don't have to do anything—you just enjoy walking on the planet Earth. The Apollo astronauts were able to take a picture of the Earth from far away and send it to us. It was the first time we saw the Earth—very beautiful—a bastion of life. The Earth is our Pure Land. It's wonderful.

If you were to go out into space, you'd see that life is something very rare. The environment of space is hostile, either very hot or very cold; it makes life impossible. Coming home to the Earth, you would feel it's wonderful to see life again—to see the plants and animals, to touch the grass with our feet, to contemplate the little flowers, to listen to the birds, to hear the wind in the branches of the pines, to observe a squirrel running up and down a tree, to breathe in and out, to get in touch with the fresh air, and to touch the earth with our feet. Many of us need to go away for seven days in order to appreciate our Pure Land when we come home to it. Many of us take it for granted. With mindfulness you'll be aware that to be present, to be alive on Earth, and to be making steps on this beautiful planet is a real miracle. Master Lin Chi said that the miracle is not to walk on water or in thin air, but the miracle is to walk on the Earth. All of us can perform the miracle of walking on the Earth; all of us can take seven steps. If we succeed, we can make the eighth step and ninth. With the energy of mindfulness, our feet become the Buddha's feet. To generate the energy of mindfulness is not difficult. The practice of mindful breathing generates the energy of mindfulness. And with that power, that energy of mindfulness, we empower our feet, and our feet become the Buddha's feet. When you walk with the feet of the Buddha, the place you walk is the Buddha land. Wherever the Buddha is, the Buddha land is there, the Pure Land is there. The Kingdom of God is always available in the here and the now; the Pure Land of the Buddha is always available. The question is, are we available to the Kingdom? Are we available to the Pure Land? Maybe we're too busy to enjoy the Pure Land, the Kingdom of God. Maybe that's why the baby Siddhartha wanted to demonstrate that he can begin to walk in the Pure Land right away after being born.

When we take refuge in the Buddha, the Dharma, and the Sangha, when we receive the Five Mindfulness Trainings, we are born again in our spiritual life, and like Siddhartha, we can make seven steps successfully. Step one, touching the Earth. Step two, feeling the sky in the Earth and so on. You need only seven steps in order to get enlightenment. Enlightenment can be realized at every moment of our daily life. To be aware that you are alive and walking on Earth—that is already enlightenment. We should reproduce that kind of enlightenment every day. Walking in the Kingdom of God, walking in the Pure Land of the Buddha is a joy—very refreshing, very healing. We know that we can do it, but very often we don't do it. We need a friend or a teacher to remind us.

Anyone can practice mindful breathing and produce mindfulness. Anyone can make a step in mindfulness and touch the earth in mindfulness, touch the Kingdom of God in mindfulness. There are those of us who need to go into outer space in order to be able to appreciate the Earth. We have the tendency to take things for granted. We don't treasure what's here already. There are so many conditions for happiness and well-being available to us, but we're not able to get in touch with them. The teaching of the Buddha is to help us to be mindful, mindful that we're there, that the sky is still blue, that the trees and the river are still there, that we can enjoy every minute of our daily life so that our continuation will have a better chance. Mindfulness makes it possible that each moment of our life becomes a wonderful moment. That is the greatest gift we can make to our children. Who are our children? Our children are ourselves, because our children are our continuation. So every moment of our daily life can become a gift to our children and to the world.

## WITH THE FEET OF THE BUDDHA

The first time I went to India, as we were coming in to land at the city of Patna, I had fifteen minutes to contemplate the landscape below. For the first time I saw the Ganges River. As a novice I had learned of the Ganges River, and of the sands of the Ganges, too numerous to count. In the old times they called Patna, Pataliputra. It was the capital of Magadha after the passing away of the Buddha. Sitting in the airplane, I looked down and I saw the footprints of the Buddha a little bit everywhere all along the Ganges River. It is certain that the Buddha walked back and forth many times along that river; there were many kingdoms centered on the river. I was very moved. Fifteen minutes to contemplate, to visualize, and to see the Buddha walking with dignity, freedom, peace, and joy. He walked like that for forty-five years, bringing his wisdom and compassion and sharing his practice of liberation with so many people—the most powerful people in the society, like kings and ministers, and the most excluded people in society like the untouchables, scavengers, and so on.

The Buddha loved walking. He walked a lot. In his time there was no car, no train, no airplane. From time to time he used a boat to go down or across a river. But mostly he walked. He walked with his friends, his disciples. During his forty-five years of teaching he visited and taught in perhaps fourteen or fifteen countries of ancient India and Nepal. Of course the Buddha enjoyed sitting meditation, but he also enjoyed walking meditation.

If you go to India and visit Benares and if from there you want to go to New Delhi, you have to fly. But the Buddha walked to Delhi. During the three-month rainy season, the Buddha stayed in one place to hold the Rains retreat with other monks. But during the other months of the year the Buddha liked to go here and there, and meet with people, and help people to practice. The layperson Anathapindika, the one who offered the Buddha the Jeta Park, had a daughter, Sunanagada, who was married to a lord who lived in the area of Bengal. One day Anathapindika's daughter asked the Buddha to come to the place where she lived. He walked to the east coast of India with 500 monks. He enjoyed the east coast and gave many teachings there. He spent more than twenty rains retreats in the Jeta Monastery. He went north to where New Delhi is today. And he went frequently to the west. The King of Avanti wanted to invite him to come to the west coast, but instead he sent two senior disciples. One of them was Mahakatyayana, and the other was Shonakutivimsa. Mahakatyayana was a skillful and eloquent Dharma teacher. They went to the west coast and set up many practice centers there. The conditions on the west coast were different, so these two monks asked the Buddha to modify some of the precepts so that the teaching could be more easily practiced on the west coast. The precepts in question had to do with footwear. The monks in the west were allowed to wear shoes of several layers to protect their feet, and they were allowed to sit on the skins of dead animals to protect themselves from humidity and from stones. The conditions of life were harsher there.

There was a rich merchant from the west coast who met the Buddha in Shravasti and who wanted to become a monk. After becoming a monk and practicing well, he wanted to go home to the west coast to set up a community. His name was Puñña. A famous conversation between the Buddha and Puñña has been recorded. The Buddha said, "I hear that the people in the west are not very gentle and get angry easily. If when you go there they were to shout at you, what would you do?" And the monk Puñña said, "Well, Lord, if they shout at me I would say that they are still compassionate because they haven't thrown rocks at me." "But what if they were to throw rocks?" "Lord, I would still think that they are compassionate enough because they aren't beating me with sticks." "What if they were to use sticks?" "Then I would still think they are compassionate because they aren't using knives to kill me." And the Buddha said, "What if they use a knife and kill you?" "In the case that I would die for the sake of the Dharma. I'd be very happy. I'm not afraid. And my death, too, would be a teaching." And the Buddha said, "Good, you are ready to go there." So the Venerable Puñña received the support of the Buddha and the community and he went to the west coast and founded a monastery and eventually there were 500 monks.

When we walk in mindfulness, our feet become the feet of the Buddha. Nowadays we can see the feet of the Buddha walking not only to the west coast of India, but also to Africa, Australia, New Zealand, Russia, and South America. Your feet have become the feet of the Buddha. Because you are there, the Buddha can go anywhere. Wherever you are, whether you're in Holland, Germany, Israel, or Canada, you walk for the Buddha. You are a friend of the Buddha, a disciple of the Buddha, a continuation of the Buddha. Thanks to you, the Buddha continues to walk and touch the Earth everywhere. Each step you make can bring about solidity, freedom, and joy. With the Buddha's feet we can bring the Buddha to the remotest areas, to slums or to impoverished areas of the countryside where there's hunger and social discrimination. You can bring the Buddha to the prisons. You make the Dharma available to everyone. I think it's very wonderful to be a continuation of the Buddha. And you know that you can do it, you can be the continuation of the Buddha—it's easy. You just breathe, you just walk, and you can continue the Buddha. When you do so, every moment of your daily life becomes a miracle.

That is the greatest gift you can make to future generations. You don't need a lot of money, or fame, or power to be happy. We need mindfulness in order to be happy. We need freedom—freedom from our worries, craving, and anxieties—so we are able to get in touch with the wonders of life that are available in the here and the now. It can be done, both individually and with the support of the Sangha. Everywhere you go you can bring the Buddha with you, because you are a continuation of the Buddha. Anywhere you go, you can set up a Sangha to support your practice, so the Buddha can stay there for a long time, and will have a chance to move ahead further.

## TOUCHING THE EARTH

Walking is a form of touching the earth. We touch the earth with our feet, and we heal the earth, we heal ourselves, and humankind. Whenever you have an extra five, ten, or fifteen minutes, enjoy walking. With every step it's possible to bring healing and nourishment to our body and to our mind. Every step taken in mindfulness with freedom can help us heal and transform, and the world will be healed and transformed together with us.

Just start like the baby Buddha and begin with seven steps. We bring ourselves home to the here and the now and make a step, "Touching the Earth, I know this planet is wonderful." Making the second step, your insight gets deeper, "Not only am I touching the Earth, but I'm touching the sky that is in the Earth, I touch the nature of interbeing." And with the third step you can touch all living beings, including our ancestors and the children that belong to the future. With every step we get enlightened. Walking like that is not hard labor, but is to produce the mindfulness, concentration, and insight that are the source of our well-being and happiness. Do you want to be a practitioner? It's easy. Just walk mindfully like the baby Buddha, in the here and the now, fully aware of the wonders of life that are available.

The practice of touching the earth is very healing. It is a way that you can have a direct conversation with the Buddha.* After three or four minutes of talking with the Buddha, we practice touching the earth not only with our feet, but with our two hands and our forehead; we touch the earth with five points. We surrender to the earth, we become one with the earth, and we invite the earth and allow the earth to embrace us and to heal us. We don't have to hold our suffering alone anymore. We ask the earth as our mother to hold us, to hold all our suffering so we can receive healing and transformation.

I hope that each of you will practice this in two ways. First, go near a

* See Thich Nhat Hanh, *Touching the Earth* (Berkeley, CA: Parallax Press, 2004).

plum tree or anywhere you like and practice touching the earth on your own. You breathe, you talk to the Buddha using the text, and you may add the things you feel in your heart. After two or three minutes of talking to the Buddha, you practice touching the earth. You can also practice collectively with your family or your Sangha. Even after practicing the first time, you can clearly see the transformation and healing. It can't be otherwise. It's like eating. Whenever you eat, you receive the nutrition from the food. There's no doubt about it. I'm sure that after one or two weeks of practice there will be transformation and healing, not only for us, but also for the people we carry within us.

The Buddha doesn't belong to the past, the Buddha belongs to the present. In celebrating Wesak, we allow the Buddha to be born in us. You should ask the question, "Who is the Buddha?" And you should be able to answer, "I am the Buddha"—because with mindfulness and concentration you become the Buddha. You know that you want to carry on the work of the Buddha.

## ONE BODY, MANY BODIES

The Buddha has a teaching about the Bodhisattva Diamond Matrix, Vajragarbha. He was preaching the teaching of interbeing. After he finished his teaching, suddenly many, many bodhisattvas came from the ten directions and they each looked exactly like Vajragarbha. They came to him and said, "Dear Bodhisattva Vajragarbha, we are also called Vajragarbha, and we also preach the teaching of interbeing everywhere." Then suddenly all the Buddhas in every corner of the universe reached out with their long, long arms and patted Vajragarbha on the head, and said, "Good, good, my son, you have done very well in teaching the teaching of interbeing." Although there were countless Buddhas reaching out with their long, long arms like that, there was no collision of their hands.

I think this means that when you are doing a good thing in one place, your good action will have a repercussion, an effect, everywhere in the cosmos. Don't worry if you feel you can only do one tiny good thing in one small corner of the cosmos. Just be a Buddha body in that one place. If you are in France, just take care of France. Don't worry about other places. There are other Buddha bodies in other places who are doing the same thing. You have to do it well here and your transformation bodies will do it well in other places. Everybody has his or her transformation bodies whether you believe it or not.

I have been away from Vietnam. But many friends of mine who have gone to Vietnam came home and reported that my presence in Vietnam is very clear, very strong. So I have plenty of transformation bodies operating there. Every thought that you produce, every word that you utter, every act that you have executed has gone out into the cosmos, and they are doing your job out there. You have countless transformation bodies that are doing the work. So make sure that only good transformation bodies are sent out in many directions.

In the Lotus Sutra, the Buddha revealed to his disciples his many transformation bodies. Before that his disciples believed that their teacher was only sitting *there*, limited in time and space, that their teacher could only last eighty years, moving around the countries along the Ganges River. But on that day, on the Gridhrakuta Mountain, Shakyamuni asked his transformation bodies to come in from different corners of the cosmos. The disciples of the Buddha began to see that their teacher is not just that body, that man sitting on the Gridhrakuta Mountain, because he had so very many transformation bodies. They could touch their teacher in the ultimate dimension, not only in the historical dimension. The practice is to touch yourself in the ultimate dimension, to touch your loved ones in the ultimate dimension and then you are free from fear, from space, and from time. You know that you have countless manifestation bodies everywhere. They will continue you, always. The disintegration of this body does not mean that you cease to be. You continue in many other forms. The teachings in the Lotus Sutra will help us to touch reality in its ultimate dimension, to have a clearer view of ourselves and of other people, of the world.

You have done something good. But it seems that no one is aware of that. Don't worry. All the Buddhas in the cosmos know about it. If you know how to look you will see that all the Buddhas are reaching out to touch your forehead, and they are saying, "Good, good, you are doing very well." That is what the sutra tries to convey to us.

Today if you have the opportunity to chop vegetables, try to cut the vegetables with the hand of your ancestors, the hand of the Buddha. Because the Buddha knows how to chop the vegetables—mindfully and joyfully. You do it for the Buddha, you do it for your ancestors. Today when you practice walking meditation, walk in such a way that you can see countless feet are making the same step with you. Use the power of visualization, and you can erase the notion of self and entities. You convey to your store consciousness the elements of wisdom that will help store to make good decisions for you, for all of us.

## BRINGING THE SANGHA WITH YOU

Each of us will continue the Buddha in his or her own way. If we practice mindfulness and concentration, we always have the Buddha, the Dharma, and the Sangha with us all the time, even if society is organized in such a way that makes living in the present moment difficult. But with the mind of love, with determination, we'll be able to bring along the Pure Land of the Buddha with us and share with many other people. If I have survived in the last thirty-nine years it is because I have always brought my Sangha along within myself. With the Sangha inside of you, you don't dry up as a separate cell.

From time to time you may like to pause, during walking or during cooking or during driving, and touch the Sangha inside. Ask, "Dear Sangha, are you still there with me?" And hear the Sangha answer, "We are always with you; we are supporting you. And we will not let you dry up as a single cell."

Aware of the Sangha within you and around you, you will have the energy to continue. Each of us has to become a torch. Each of us has to become an element of inspiration for many others; each of us has to be a bodhisattva. To be a bodhisattva is not something spectacular. It is our daily practice.

It's very clear in the Buddhist teachings that a Buddha is a living being. If the living being is not there, the Buddha cannot be there. In order to be a Buddha, you need to be a living being. And in order to be a living being, you need to be a Buddha, because these two are one. If the Buddha nature were not in you, you would not be a living being. Every living being has the Buddha nature. It is possible to breathe like a Buddha, to walk like a Buddha, to sit like a Buddha, and to eat and drink like a Buddha. The practice of mindfulness helps us to become the Buddha in the here and the now. If you're looking for the Buddha 2,600 years ago, you'll miss him. But if you breathe in and become enlightened about the fact that you are the Buddha, you are his continuation, then the Buddha is available right away.

The end of one journey is the beginning of the continuation. And I hope, I pray to the Buddha and all the bodhisattvas to keep you safe, healthy, and happy. We rely on you, and the Buddha relies on every one of us. Please enjoy walking today. Just take seven steps and see what happens.

# 9

## Exercises for Nourishing
## A Buddha Body and A Buddha Mind

HERE ARE some simple exercises you can do to reinforce the connection between your Buddha body and Buddha mind.

### WALKING MEDITATION*

*The mind can go in a thousand directions.*
*But on this beautiful path, I walk in peace.*
*With each step, a gentle wind blows.*
*With each step, a flower blooms.*

Walking meditation is meditation while walking. We walk slowly, in a relaxed way, keeping a light smile on our lips. When we practice this way, we feel deeply at ease, and our steps are those of the most secure person on Earth. Walking meditation is really to enjoy the walking—walking not in order to arrive, just for walking, to be in the present moment, and to enjoy each step. Therefore you have to shake off all worries and anxieties, not thinking of the future, not thinking of the past, just enjoying the present moment. Anyone can do it. It takes only a little time, a little mindfulness, and the wish to be happy.

We walk all the time, but usually it is more like running. Our hurried

---

* From *The Long Road Turns to Joy* (Berkeley, CA: Parallax Press, 1996) and *Present Moment, Wonderful Moment* (Parallax Press, 1990).

steps print anxiety and sorrow on the Earth. If we can take one step in peace, we can take two, three, four, and then five steps for the peace and happiness of humankind.

Our mind darts from one thing to another, like a monkey swinging from branch to branch without stopping to rest. Thoughts have millions of pathways, and we are forever pulled along by them into the world of forgetfulness. If we can transform our walking path into a field for meditation, our feet will take every step in full awareness, our breathing will be in harmony with our steps, and our mind will naturally be at ease. Every step we take will reinforce our peace and joy and cause a stream of calm energy to flow through us. Then we can say, "With each step, a gentle wind blows."

While walking, practice conscious breathing by counting steps. Notice each breath and the number of steps you take as you breathe in and as you breathe out. If you take three steps during an in-breath, say, silently, "One, two, three," or "In, in, in," one word with each step. As you breathe out, if you take three steps, say, "Out, out, out," with each step. If you take three steps as you breathe in and four steps as you breathe out, you say, "In, in, in. Out, out, out, out," or "One, two, three. One, two, three, four."

Don't try to control your breathing. Allow your lungs as much time and air as they need, and simply notice how many steps you take as your lungs fill up and how many you take as they empty, mindful of both your breath and your steps. The key is mindfulness.

When you walk uphill or downhill, the number of steps per breath will change. Always follow the needs of your lungs. Do not try to control your breathing or your walking. Just observe them deeply.

When you begin to practice, your exhalation may be longer than your inhalation. You might find that you take three steps during your in-breath and four steps on your out-breath (3-4), or two steps/three steps (2-3). If this is comfortable for you, please enjoy practicing this way. After you have been doing walking meditation for some time, your in-breath and out-breath will probably become equal: 3-3, or 2-2, or 4-4.

If you see something along the way that you want to touch with your mindfulness—the blue sky, the hills, a tree, or a bird—just stop, but while you do, continue breathing mindfully. You can keep the object of your contemplation alive by means of mindful breathing. If you don't breathe consciously, sooner or later your thinking will settle back in, and the bird or the tree will disappear. Always stay with your breathing.

When you walk, you might like to take the hand of a child. She will receive your concentration and stability, and you will receive her freshness and innocence. From time to time, she may want to run ahead and then wait for you to catch up. A child is a bell of mindfulness, reminding us how wonderful life is. At Plum Village, I teach the young people a simple verse to practice while walking: "Yes, yes, yes" as they breathe in, and, "Thanks, thanks, thanks" as they breathe out. I want them to respond to life, to society, and to the Earth in a positive way. They enjoy it very much.

After you have been practicing for a few days, try adding one more step to your exhalation. For example, if your normal breathing is 2-2, without walking any faster, lengthen your exhalation and practice 2-3 for four or five times. Then go back to 2-2. In normal breathing, we never expel all the air from our lungs. There is always some left. By adding another step to your exhalation, you will push out more of this stale air. Don't overdo it. Four or five times are enough. More can make you tired. After breathing this way four or five times, let your breath return to normal. Then, five or ten minutes later, you can repeat the process. Remember to add a step to the exhalation, not the inhalation.

After practicing for a few more days, your lungs might say to you, "If we could do 3-3 instead of 2-3, that would be wonderful." If the message is clear, try it, but even then, only do it four or five times. Then go back to 2-2. In five or ten minutes, begin 2-3, and then do 3-3 again. After several months, your lungs will be healthier and your blood will circulate better. Your way of breathing will have been transformed.

When we practice walking meditation, we arrive in each moment. When we enter the present moment deeply, our regrets and sorrows disappear, and we discover life with all its wonders. Breathing in, we say to ourselves, "I have arrived." Breathing out, we say, "I am home." When we do this, we overcome dispersion and dwell peacefully in the present moment, which is the only moment for us to be alive.

You can also practice walking meditation using the lines of a poem. In Zen Buddhism, poetry and practice always go together.

> *I have arrived.*
> *I am home*
> *in the here,*
> *in the now.*
> *I am solid.*
> *I am free.*
> *In the ultimate*
> *I dwell.*

As you walk, be fully aware of your foot, the ground, and the connection between them, which is your conscious breathing. People say that walking on water is a miracle, but to me, walking peacefully on the Earth is the real miracle. The Earth is a miracle. Each step is a miracle. Taking steps on our beautiful planet can bring real happiness.

## TOUCHING THE EARTH

The practice of Touching the Earth is to return to the Earth, to our roots, to our ancestors, and to recognize that we are not alone but connected to a whole stream of spiritual and blood ancestors. We are their continuation, and with them we will continue in future generations. We touch the earth to let go of the idea that we are separate and to remind us that we are the Earth and part of life.

When we touch the earth we become small, with the humility and simplicity of a young child. When we touch the Earth we become great, like an ancient tree sending her roots deep into the earth, drinking from the source of all waters. When we touch the earth, we breathe in all the strength and stability of the earth, and breathe out our suffering—our feelings of anger, hatred, fear, inadequacy, and grief.

We join our palms to form a lotus bud and we gently lower ourselves to the ground so that all four limbs and our forehead are resting comfortably on the floor. While we are Touching the Earth we turn our palms face up, showing our openness to the Three Jewels—the Buddha, the Dharma, and the Sangha. Even after practicing the *Five Touchings* or the *Three Touchings* only one or two times, we can already release a lot of our suffering and feeling of alienation and reconcile with our ancestors, parents, children, friends.

## The Five Earth-Touchings

I

In gratitude, I bow to all generations of ancestors in my blood family.
[BELL]
[ALL TOUCH THE EARTH]

I see my mother and father, whose blood, flesh, and vitality are circulating in my own veins and nourishing every cell in me. Through them, I see my four grandparents. Their expectations, experiences, and wisdom have been transmitted from so many generations of ancestors. I carry in me the life, blood, experience, wisdom, happiness, and sorrow of all generations. The suffering and all the elements that need to be transformed, I am practicing to transform. I open my heart, flesh, and bones to receive the energy of insight, love, and experience transmitted to me by all my ancestors. I see my roots in my father, mother, grandfathers, grandmothers, and all my ancestors. I know I am only the continuation of this ancestral lineage. Please support, protect, and transmit to me your energy. I know wherever children and grandchildren are, ancestors are there, also. I know that parents always love and support their children and grandchildren, although they are not always able to express it skillfully because of difficulties they themselves encountered. I see that my ancestors tried to build a way of life based on gratitude, joy, confidence, respect, and loving kindness. As a continuation of my ancestors, I bow deeply and allow their energy to flow through me. I ask my ancestors for their support, protection, and strength.
[THREE BREATHS]
[BELL]

## II
In gratitude, I bow to all generations of ancestors in my spiritual family.
[BELL]
[ALL TOUCH THE EARTH]

I see in myself my teachers, the ones who show me the way of love and understanding, the way to breathe, smile, forgive, and live deeply in the present moment. I see through my teachers all teachers over many generations and traditions, going back to the ones who began my spiritual family thousands of years ago. I see the Buddha or Christ or the patriarchs and matriarchs as my teachers, and also as my spiritual ancestors. I see that their energy and that of many generations of teachers has entered me and is creating peace, joy, understanding, and loving kindness in me. I know that the energy of these teachers has deeply transformed the world. Without the Buddha and all these spiritual ancestors, I would not know the way to practice to bring peace and happiness into my life and into the lives of my family and society. I open my heart and my body to receive the energy of understanding, loving kindness, and protection from the Awakened Ones, their teachings, and the community of practice over many generations. I am their continuation. I ask these spiritual ancestors to transmit to me their infinite source of energy, peace, stability, understanding, and love. I vow to practice to transform the suffering in myself and the world, and to transmit their energy to future generations of practitioners. My spiritual ancestors may have had their own difficulties and not always been able to transmit the teachings, but I accept them as they are.
[THREE BREATHS]
[BELL]
[ALL STAND UP]

## III
In gratitude, I bow to this land and all of the ancestors who
made it available.*

---

* Substitute the names of ancestors appropriate for the country in which you are practicing.

[BELL]
[ALL TOUCH THE EARTH]

I see that I am whole, protected, and nourished by this land and all of the living beings who have been here and made life easy and possible for me through all their efforts. I see Chief Seattle, Thomas Jefferson, Dorothy Day, Cesar Chavez, Martin Luther King, Jr., and all the others known and unknown. I see all those who have made this country a refuge for people of so many origins and colors, by their talent, perseverance, and love—those who have worked hard to build schools, hospitals, bridges, and roads, to protect human rights, to develop science and technology, and to fight for freedom and social justice. I see myself touching my ancestors of Native American origin who have lived on this land for such a long time and known the ways to live in peace and harmony with nature, protecting the mountains, forests, animals, vegetation, and minerals of this land. I feel the energy of this land penetrating my body and soul, supporting and accepting me. I vow to cultivate and maintain this energy and transmit it to future generations. I vow to contribute my part in transforming the violence, hatred, and delusion that still lie deep in the collective consciousness of this society so that future generations will have more safety, joy, and peace. I ask this land for its protection and support.
[THREE BREATHS]
[BELL]
[ALL STAND UP]

**IV**
In gratitude and compassion, I bow down and transmit my energy
to those I love.
[BELL]
[ALL TOUCH THE EARTH]

All the energy I have received I now want to transmit to my father, my mother, everyone I love, all who have suffered and worried because of me and for my sake. I know I have not been mindful enough in my daily life. I also know that those who love me have had their own difficulties. They have suffered because they were not lucky enough to have an environment that encouraged their full development. I transmit my energy to my mother, my father, my brothers, my sisters, my beloved ones, my husband, my wife, my daughter, and my son, so that their pain will be relieved, so they can smile and feel the joy of being alive. I want all of them to be healthy and joyful. I know that when they are happy, I will also be happy. I no longer feel resentment towards any of them. I pray that all ancestors in my blood and spiritual families will focus their energies toward each of them, to protect and support them. I know that I am not separate from them. I am one with those I love.

[THREE BREATHS]

[BELL]

[ALL STAND UP]


V

In understanding and compassion, I bow down to reconcile myself with all those who have made me suffer.

[BELL]

[ALL TOUCH THE EARTH]


I open my heart and send forth my energy of love and understanding to everyone who has made me suffer, to those who have destroyed much of my life and the lives of those I love. I know now that these people have themselves undergone a lot of suffering and that their hearts are overloaded with pain, anger, and hatred. I know that anyone who suffers that much will make those around him or her suffer. I know they may have been unlucky, never having the chance to be cared for and loved. Life and society have dealt them so many hardships. They have been wronged and abused. They have not been guided in the path of mindful living. They have accumulated wrong perceptions about life, about me, and about us. They have wronged us and the people we love. I pray to my ancestors in my blood and spiritual families to channel to these persons who have made us suffer the energy of love and protection, so that their hearts will be able to receive the nectar of love and blossom like a flower. I pray that they can be transformed to experience the joy of living, so that they will not continue to make themselves and others suffer. I see their suffering and do not want to hold any feelings of hatred or anger in myself toward them. I do not want them to suffer. I channel my energy of love and understanding to them and ask all my ancestors to help them.

[THREE BREATHS]

[BELL]

[ALL STAND UP]


## The Three Earth-Touchings

I

Touching the Earth, I connect with ancestors and descendants of both my spiritual and my blood families.

[BELL]

[ALL TOUCH THE EARTH]


My spiritual ancestors include the Buddha, the Bodhisattvas, the noble Sangha of Buddha's disciples, [INSERT NAMES OF OTHERS YOU WOULD LIKE TO INCLUDE], and my own spiritual teachers still alive or already passed away. They are present in me because they have transmitted to me seeds of peace, wisdom, love, and happiness. They have woken up in me my resource of understanding and compassion. When I look at my spiritual ancestors, I see those who are perfect in the practice of the mindfulness trainings, understanding, and compassion, and those who are still imperfect. I accept them all because I see within myself shortcomings and weaknesses. Aware that my practice of the mindfulness trainings is not always perfect, and that I am not always as understanding and compassionate as I would like to be, I open my heart and accept all my spiritual descendants. Some of my descendants practice the mindfulness trainings, understanding, and compassion in a way which invites confidence and respect, but there are also those who come across many difficulties and are constantly subject to ups and downs in their practice.

In the same way, I accept all my ancestors on my mother's side and my father's side of the family. I accept all their good qualities and their virtuous actions, and I also accept all their weaknesses. I open my heart and accept all my blood descendants with their good qualities, their talents, and also their weaknesses.

My spiritual ancestors, blood ancestors, spiritual descendants, and blood descendants are all part of me. I am them, and they are me. I do not have a separate self. All exist as part of a wonderful stream of life which is constantly moving.

[THREE BREATHS]

[BELL]

[ALL STAND UP]


## II

Touching the Earth, I connect with all people and all species that are alive at this moment in this world with me.

[BELL]

[ALL TOUCH THE EARTH]


I am one with the wonderful pattern of life that radiates out in all directions. I see the close connection between myself and others, how we share happiness and suffering. I am one with those who were born disabled or who have become disabled because of war, accident, or illness. I am one with those who are caught in a situation of war or oppression. I am one with those who find no happiness in family life, who have no roots and no peace of mind, who are hungry for understanding and love, and who are looking for something beautiful, wholesome, and true to embrace and to believe in. I am someone at the point of death who is very afraid and does not know what is going to happen. I am a child who lives in a place where there is miserable poverty and disease, whose legs and arms are like sticks and who has no future. I am also the manufacturer of bombs that are sold to poor countries. I am the frog swimming in the pond and I am also the snake who needs the body of the frog to nourish its own body. I am the caterpillar or the ant that the bird is looking for to eat, and I am also the bird that is looking for the caterpillar or the ant. I am the forest that is being cut down. I am the rivers and the air that are being polluted, and I am also the person who cuts down the forest and pollutes the rivers and the air. I see myself in all species, and I see all species in me.

I am one with the great beings who have realized the truth of no-birth and no-death and are able to look at the forms of birth and death, happiness and suffering, with calm eyes. I am one with those people—who can be found a little bit everywhere—who have sufficient peace of mind, understanding and love, who are able to touch what is wonderful, nourishing, and healing, who also have the capacity to embrace the world with a heart of love and arms of caring action. I am someone who has enough peace, joy, and freedom and is able to offer fearlessness and joy to living beings around themselves. I see that I am not lonely and cut off. The love and the happiness of great beings on this planet help me not to sink in despair. They help me to live my life in a meaningful way, with true peace and happiness. I see them all in me, and I see myself in all of them.

[THREE BREATHS]

[BELL]

[ALL STAND UP]


## III

Touching the Earth, I let go of my idea that I am this body and my life span is limited.

[BELL]

[ALL TOUCH THE EARTH]


I see that this body, made up of the four elements, is not really me and I am not limited by this body. I am part of a stream of life of spiritual and blood ancestors that for thousands of years has been flowing into the present and flows on for thousands of years into the future. I am one with my ancestors. I am one with all people and all species, whether they are peaceful and fearless, or suffering and afraid. At this very moment, I am present everywhere on this planet. I am also present in the past and in the future. The disintegration of this body does not touch me, just as when the plum blossom falls it does not mean the end of the plum tree. I see myself as a wave on the surface of the ocean. My nature is the ocean water. I see myself in all the other waves and see all the other waves in me. The appearance and disappearance of the form of the wave does not affect the ocean. My Dharma body and spiritual life are not subject to birth and death. I see the presence of myself before my body manifested and after my body has disintegrated. Even in this moment, I see how I exist elsewhere than in this body. Seventy or eighty years is not my life span. My life span, like the life span of a leaf or of a Buddha, is limitless. I have gone beyond the idea that I am a body that is separated in space and time from all other forms of life.

[THREE BREATHS]

[BELL]

[ALL STAND UP]

## DEEP RELAXATION

Resting is a precondition for healing. When animals in the forest get wounded, they find a place to lie down, and they rest completely for many days. They don't think about food or anything else. They just rest, and they get the healing they need. When we humans become overcome with stress, we may go to the pharmacy and get drugs, but we don't stop. We don't know how to help ourselves.

Stess accumulates in our body. The way we eat, drink, and live takes its toll on our well-being. Deep relaxation is an opportunity for our body to rest, to heal, and be restored. We relax our body, give our attention to each part in turn, and send our love and care to every cell.

Mindful breathing, total relaxation of the body can be done at home at least once a day. It may last for twenty minutes or longer. The living room can be used to practice total relaxation. One member of the family can lead the session of total relaxation. And the young people can learn how to lead a session of total relaxation for the whole family.

I think in the twenty-first century we have to set up a hall for total relaxation in school. If you are a school teacher, you can master the techniques and invite your students to practice it before class or half way through the class, in a sitting position or a lying position. Teachers and students can enjoy practicing mindful breathing and total relaxation together. This helps the teachers have less stress, and it helps the students and brings the spiritual dimension into the school. If you are a doctor you can master the techniques and help your patients. If your patients know the art of mindful breathing and total relaxation, their capacity of healing themselves will increase and the process of healing will take place more quickly. In the National Assembly, in the Congress, the members can also practice total relaxation and mindful breathing. Sometimes the debates in the Parliament can go late into the night. Many members are under stress. We want our Parliament to be relaxed, to feel well, in order to make the best decision they can make. This is a practice that is not sectarian or religious; it's scientific. One session of practice can already bring good results to everyone that practices. It's very important to practice deep relaxation.

If you have trouble sleeping enough, deep relaxation can compensate. Lying awake on your bed, you may like to practice total relaxation and follow your breathing in and breathing out. Sometimes it can help you to get some sleep. But even if you don't sleep, the practice is still very good because it can nourish you and allow you to rest. You can also listen to beautiful chanting; that can help very much with releasing and nourishing. It's very important to allow yourself to rest.

When we do deep relaxation in a group, one person can guide the exercise using the following cues or some variation of them. When you do deep relaxation on your own, you may like to record an exercise to follow as you practice.

## Deep Relaxation Exercise

Lie down on your back with your arms at your sides. Make yourself comfortable. Allow your body to relax. Be aware of the floor underneath you...and of the contact of your body with the floor. (Pause) Allow your body to sink into the floor. (Pause)

Become aware of your breathing, in and out. Be aware of your abdomen rising and falling as you breathe in and out…rising…falling…rising…falling. (Pause)

Breathing in, bring your awareness to your eyes. Breathing out, allow your eyes to relax. Allow your eyes to sink back into your head…let go of the tension in all the tiny muscles around your eyes…our eyes allow us to see a paradise of form and color…allow your eyes to rest…send love and gratitude to your eyes. (Pause)

Breathing in, bring your awareness to your mouth. Breathing out, allow your mouth to relax. Release the tension around your mouth…your lips are the petals of a flower…let a gentle smile bloom on your lips…smiling releases the tension in the hundreds of muscles in your face…feel the tension release in your cheeks…your jaw…your throat. (Pause)

Breathing in, bring your awareness to your shoulders. Breathing out, allow your shoulders to relax. Let them sink into the floor…let all the accumulated tension flow into the floor…we carry so much with our shoulders…now let them relax as we care for our shoulders. (Pause)

Breathing in, become aware of your arms. Breathing out, relax your arms. Let your arms sink into the floor…your upper arms…your elbows…your lower arms…your wrists…hands…fingers…all the tiny muscles…move your fingers a little if you need to, to help the muscles relax. (Pause)

Breathing in, bring your awareness to your heart. Breathing out, allow your heart to relax. (Pause) We have neglected our heart for a long time… by the way we work, eat, and manage anxiety and stress. (Pause) Our heart beats for us night and day…embrace your heart with mindfulness and tenderness…reconciling and taking care of your heart. (Pause)

Breathing in, bring your awareness to your legs. Breathing out, allow your legs to relax. Release all the tension in your legs…your thighs…your knees…your calves…your ankles…your feet…your toes…all the tiny muscles in your toes…you may want to move your toes a little to help them relax…send your love and care to your toes. (Pause)

Breathing in, breathing out…my whole body feels light …like duck weed floating on the water…I have nowhere to go…nothing to do…I am relax...send your love and care to your toes. (Pause)

Breathing in, breathing out...my whole body feels light...like duck weed floating on the water...I have nowhere to go...nothing to do...I am free as the cloud floating in the sky. (Pause)

(Singing or music for some minutes) (Pause)

Bring your awareness back to your breathing...to your abdomen rising and falling. (Pause)

Following your breathing, become aware of your arms and legs...you may want to move them a little and stretch. (Pause)

When you feel ready, slowly sit up. (Pause)

When you are ready, slowly stand up.

In the above exercise can guide awareness to any part of the body: the hair, scalp, brain, ears, neck, lungs, each of the internal organs, the digestive system, pelvis, and to any part of the body that needs healing and attention, embracing each part and sending love, gratitude, and care as we hold it in our awareness and breathe in and out.

# The Verses on the Characteristics of the Eight Consciousnesses

## 八識規矩頌

BY MASTER HSÜAN-TSANG    (ca. 596–664 C.E.)
OF THE TANG DYNASTY IN CHINA
*Translated from Chinese by Thich Nhat Hanh*

### VERSE ON THE FIRST FIVE CONSCIOUSNESSES

性境現量通三性， 眼耳身三二地居；
徧行別境善十一， 中二大八貪瞋癡。

The object of the first five consciousnesses is the sphere of nature, their mode of cognition is direct, and their nature can either be wholesome, unwholesome or neutral. In the Second Land, only eye consciousness, ear consciousness and body consciousness operate. The five sense consciousnesses operate with the five Universals, the five Particulars, the eleven Wholesome mental formations, the two Middle Secondary Unwholesome mental formations (lack of inner shame, lack of shame before others), the eight Greater Secondary mental formations, and with craving, hatred, and confusion.

五識同依淨色根， 九緣七八好相鄰；
合三離二觀塵世， 愚者難分識與根。

All five consciousnesses operate on the ground of Pure Sense Organs, depending on nine, eight or seven conditions. They observe the world of dust; two of them from a distance, three from direct contact. Naïve people find it difficult to distinguish between organ and consciousness.

變相觀空唯後得，果中猶自不詮真；
圓明初發成無漏，三類分身息苦輪。

It is thanks to Later Acquired Wisdom that the five consciousnesses could contemplate emptiness in its manifested forms. Therefore even after enlightenment, the five consciousnesses by themselves are still not capable of reaching out to true emptiness. When the eighth consciousness is transformed into the Great Mirror Wisdom, the five sense consciousnesses can attain the state of "no-leaking" (*anasvara*). Thereupon, the three types of manifestation bodies are available to help us end the cycle of suffering in the world.

## VERSE ON THE SIXTH CONSCIOUSNESS

三性三量通三境，三界輪時易可知；
相應心所五十一，善惡臨時別配之。

The sixth consciousness can be easily observed when it operates in the three natures, the three modes of cognition, and the three kinds of objects of cognition, and when it still goes around in the three realms. This consciousness operates with all the fifty-one mental formations. Whether wholesome or unwholesome, its nature depends on times and occasions.

性界受三恒轉易，根隨信等總相連；
動身發語獨爲最，引滿能招業力牽。

Related to the sixth consciousness, the three natures, the three realms, and the three feelings are in permanent transformation and change. The six Primary Unwholesome mental formations, the twenty Secondary Unwholesome mental formations, and the eleven Wholesome mental formations (such as faith etc.) all are related. The sixth consciousness constitutes the main dynamic force for speech and action that will determine future retribution in both general and particular terms.

發起初心歡喜地, 俱生猶自現纏眠;
遠行地後純無漏, 觀察圓明照大千。。

Even when the practitioner enters the Land of Joy with her bodhisattva's beginner's mind, the innate attachment to a self still lies dormant in the depths of her consciousness. It is only when she reaches the Seventh Land, called the Land of Far Reaching, that this consciousness is free from "leaks." At this time, the sixth consciousness becomes the Wisdom of Wonderful Contemplation, illuminating the whole cosmos.

## VERSE ON THE SEVENTH CONSCIOUSNESS

帶質有覆通情本, 隨緣執我量爲非;
八大偏行別境慧, 貪癡我見慢相隨。

Obscured, with an object that carries some substance linking the Lover and the Base, the seventh consciousness always follows and clings to the Base as a self. Its mode of cognition is erroneous. It operates with the five Universals, the eight Greater Secondary mental formations, with *mati* (one of the five Particulars) and with self-love (貪, craving), self-delusion (癡, ignorance), self-view (見, [wrong] view), and self-conceit (慢, arrogance).

恒審思量我相隨, 有情日夜鎮昏迷;
四惑八大相應起, 六轉呼爲染淨依。

Continuously following and grasping the object of self, this consciousness induces the state of dreaming and confusion in living beings day and night. The four afflictions and the eight Greater Secondary mental formations always manifest and operate with the seventh consciousness. This consciousness is also called the ground of defilement and purity for the other six evolving consciousnesses.

極喜初心平等性，無功用行我恒摧；
如來現起他受用，十地菩薩所被機。

When the practitioner reaches the Land of Extreme Joy, the nature of equanimity begins to reveal itself. When he arrives at the Eighth Land, the Land of Effortlessness, the illusion of self is gone. At this time, the Tathagatha manifests His body for the sake of others, and all the bodhisattvas of the ten lands benefit from his presence.

## VERSE ON THE EIGHTH (STORE) CONSCIOUSNESS

性唯無覆五徧行，界地隨他業力生；
二乘不了因迷執，由此能興論主諍。

With its indeterminate (and non-obscuring) nature, the eighth consciousness operates with the five Universals. Realms and Lands depend on karmic power. People belonging to the lesser Vehicles do not know about the eighth consciousness because of their attachment and wrong views. It is for this reason that they still debate about its presence.

浩浩三藏不可窮，淵深七浪境爲風；
受熏持種根身器，去後來先作主翁。

How immense is the Unfathomable Triple Store! From the deep ocean of the Store arise the seven waves of the seven evolving consciousnesses, the wind being the object of their cognition! This consciousness receives impregnation, preserves all seeds and also the body, organs, and environment. It is the one who comes first and leaves last, being truly a master of the house!

不動地前纔捨藏，金剛道後異熟空；
大圓無垢同時發，普照十方塵刹中！

Before arriving at the Land of Immovability, the function of the eighth consciousness is abandoned. After reaching the Diamond Path, there is no more retribution. The Great Mirror Wisdom and the Immaculate Consciousness appear at the same time, illuminating the innumerable Buddha fields in the ten directions.

# Fifty-one Mental Formations

| SANSKRIT | ENGLISH |
| --- | --- |
| **sarvatraga** | **5 Universals** |
| sparsa | contact |
| manaskara | attention |
| vedana | feeling |
| samjna | perception |
| cetana | volition |
| **viniyata** | **5 Particulars** |
| chanda | intention |
| adhimoksa | determination |
| smrti | mindfulness |
| samadhi | concentration |
| prajna (mati) | insight |
| **kusala 11** | **Wholesome** |
| sraddha | faith |
| hri | inner shame |
| apatrapya | shame before others |
| alobha | absence of craving |

| | |
|---|---|
| advesa | absence of hatred |
| amoha | absence of ignorance |
| virya | diligence, energy |
| prasjbdhi | tranquility, ease |
| apramada | vigilance, energy |
| upeksa | equanimity |
| ahimsa | non-harming |

| | **Wholesome mental formations added by Thich Nhat Hanh** |
|---|---|
| abhaya | non-fear |
| asoka | absence of anxiety |
| sthira | stability, solidity |
| maitri | loving kindness |
| karuna | compassion |
| mudita | joy |
| sagauravata | humility |
| sukha | happiness |
| nirjvara | feverlessness |
| vasika | freedom/sovereignty |

| **klesa** | **6 Primary Unwholesome** |
|---|---|
| raga | craving, covetousness |
| pratigha | hatred |
| mudhi | ignorance, confusion |
| mana | arrogance |
| vicikitsa | doubt, suspicion |
| drsti | wrong view |

| upaklesa | 20 Secondary Unwholesome |
|---|---|
| | 10 MINOR SECONDARY UNWHOLESOME |
| krodha | anger |
| upanaha | resentment, enmity |
| mraksa | concealment |
| pradasa | maliciousness |
| irsya | jealousy |
| matsarya | selfishness, parsimony |
| maya | deceitfulness, fraud |
| sathya | guile |
| vihimsa | desire to harm |
| mada | pride |
| | 2 MIDDLE SECONDARY UNWHOLESOME |
| ahrikya | lack of inner shame |
| anapatrapya | lack of shame before others |
| | 8 GREATER SECONDARY UNWHOLESOME |
| auddhatya | restlessness |
| styana | drowsiness |
| sraddhya | lack of faith, unbelief |
| pramada | laziness |
| kausidya | negligence |
| musitasmrtita | forgetfulness |
| viksepa | distraction |
| samprajna | lack of discernment |

|  | Unwholesome mental formations added by Thich Nhat Hanh |
| --- | --- |
| bhaya | fear |
| soka | anxiety |
| visada | despair |

| **aniyata 4** | **Indeterminate** |
| --- | --- |
| kaukytya | regret, repentance |
| middha | sleepiness |
| vitarka | initial thought |
| vicara | sustained thought |

Parallax Press, a nonprofit organization, publishes books on engaged Buddhism and the practice of mindfulness by Thich Nhat Hanh and other authors. All of Thich Nhat Hanh's work is available at our online store and in our free catalog. For a copy of the catalog, please contact:

Parallax Press
P.O. Box 7355
Berkeley, CA 94707
Tel: (510) 525-0101
**www.parallax.org**

Monastics and laypeople practice the art of mindful living in the tradition of Thich Nhat Hanh at retreat communities in France and the United States. To reach any of these communities, or for information about individuals and families joining for a practice period, please contact:

Plum Village
13 Martineau
33580 Dieulivol, France
**www.plumvillage.org**

Blue Cliff Monastery
3 Hotel Road
Pine Bush, NY 12566
**www.bluecliffmonastery.org**

Deer Park Monastery
2499 Melru Lane
Escondido, CA 92026
**www.deerparkmonastery.org**

*The Mindfulness Bell*, a Journal of the Art of Mindful Living in the Tradition of Thich Nhat Hanh, is published three times a year by Plum Village. To subscribe or see the worldwide directory of Sanghas, visit www.mindfulnessbell.org